John Birkenhead

Ferns and Fern Culture

Selections of Ferns

John Birkenhead

Ferns and Fern Culture
Selections of Ferns

ISBN/EAN: 9783337049850

Printed in Europe, USA, Canada, Australia, Japan

Cover: Foto ©Lupo / pixelio.de

More available books at **www.hansebooks.com**

FERNS

AND

FERN CULTURE:

THEIR NATIVE HABITATS, ORGANISATION, HABITS
OF GROWTH, COMPOST FOR DIFFERENT
GENERA; CULTIVATION IN POTS,
BASKETS, ROCKWORK, WALLS;

IN

STOVE, GREENHOUSE, DWELLING-
HOUSE, AND OUTDOOR FERNERIES;
POTTING, WATERING, PROPAGATION, ETC.

SELECTIONS OF FERNS

SUITABLE FOR STOVE, WARM, COOL, AND COLD GREEN-
HOUSES; FOR BASKETS, WALLS, EXHIBITION,
WARDIAN CASES, DWELLING-HOUSES,
AND OUTDOOR FERNERIES.

INSECT PESTS AND THEIR ERADICATION, &c.

BY

J. BIRKENHEAD, F.R.H.S.

PRICE ONE SHILLING. By Post, 1s. 3d.

May be had from the AUTHOR, Fern Nursery, Sale, Manchester.
Also from
JOHN HEYWOOD, Bookseller, Manchester;
W. H. SMITH & Sons, Booksellers, Manchester.

CONTENTS.

———※———

	PAGE.
PREFACE	5
FERNS AND FERN CULTURE	7

SECTION 1.
    Geographical Distribution of Ferns... 9
    Rules for Fern Culture 10
    Modes of Growth—Roots, Stems, Fronds ... 11

SECTION 2.
    Compost, Loam, Leaf Mould, Peat, Sand, Sandstone, Charcoal, Moss, Crocks, Potting Sticks   25

SECTION 3.
    Compost for various Genera 30
    Do.   do.   in Pots, Wardian Cases, Walls, Pockets, Rockwork 33

SECTION 4.
    Habits of Ferns 34

SECTION 5.
    Various Modes of Cultivation 44
    Potting, Baskets, Hanging Blocks of Cork   46
    Ferns in Rockwork, Moss-covered Walls ... 54
    Walls Covered with Cork, Wall Tiles ... 55
    Rockwork (Indoors) 56
    Outdoor Ferneries... 57
    Rock Fernery with Glass Protection ... 61

SECTION 6.
    Light, Means of Shading 63

Contents.

SECTION 7.   PAGE.

Temperature, Ventilation, Watering   66
Moisture in the Atmosphere, Cutting Ferns Down   70

SECTION 8.

Ferns in Dwelling-houses, Wardian Cases, Fern
Stands, Window Boxes, Window Cases... ...   72

SECTION 9.

Propagation by Bulbils, Division of Rhizomes,
Division of Crowns, Spores   78

SECTION 10.

Selections of Stove Ferns for Pots, Baskets, Blocks
of Cork, Rockwork, Walls, Cutting   85
Stove Selaginellas   91
Selections of Warm Greenhouse Ferns for Pots,
Baskets, Blocks of Cork, Rockwork, Walls,
Cutting   92
Warm Greenhouse Selaginellas   97
Selections of Cool Greenhouse Ferns for Pots,
Baskets, Blocks of Cork, Walls, Cutting ...   98
Cool Greenhouse Selaginellas   101
Selections of Cold Greenhouse Ferns for Pots,
Baskets, Walls, Cutting   102
Cold Greenhouse Selaginellas   106
Filmy Ferns for Cool and Cold Greenhouses ...   106
Exhibition Ferns — Stove. Greenhouse, Hardy
Exotic, British (dwarf), British (large) ...   109
Ferns for Dwelling-house, Fern Stands, Wardian
Cases, Window Cases, Window Boxes ...   112
Tree-Ferns for Greenhouses   115
Ferns for Outdoor Ferneries   115

SECTION 11.

Insect Pests and their Eradication   123

PREFACE.

FERNS are now in great demand for cultivation in greenhouses, dwelling-houses, and out-door ferneries; also for decoration on special occasions and for cutting. Amateurs in every position of life are taking interest in, and are desirous of cultivating, these plants. The demand for information as to the best kinds to procure, and the proper way to treat them, is so great, that this treatise has been prepared, and it is sent forth in the hope that it may help all its readers to obtain the best results in their efforts to cultivate these beautiful plants.

The aim of the author has been to give simple and clear instructions — avoiding, as far as possible, technical phraseology—and to supply all necessary information, interspersing here and there such remarks as it is hoped may add to the interest and benefit of perusal.

It is not intended for the book to count as a botanical or scientific production, but simply as a practical guide.

The various subjects are necessarily treated briefly, but as the information given is the result of twenty-five years' experience in the cultivation of Ferns, and in the daily study of their requirements, the writer trusts that the remarks, though brief, may prove lucid enough even for the most inexperienced amateur to understand and profit by.

JOHN BIRKENHEAD.

Sale, May, 1892.

FERNS AND FERN CULTURE.

T is safe to say there is no class of plants which, taken the year round, gives such continued pleasure and combines such grace, beauty, and utility as Ferns.

It is true they are flowerless plants; nevertheless, they are nearly everybody's favourites. Without introducing an odious comparison, it may be said that orchids, roses, begonias, and other popular plants are attractive and much admired when in flower, yet, when not in flower, they are most unattractive and uninteresting in appearance, but Ferns are always beautiful.

Even those who do not take special interest in Ferns readily acknowledge that flowering plants, or flowers in a cut state, are greatly improved by association with Ferns. As, however, this is not intended to be a plea for Fern culture, but a guide thereto, these remarks will suffice on this point.

The vegetable kingdom is divided into two sections, one consisting of flowering plants, the other of those which are flowerless. Ferns are placed at the head of the latter class. They are of great antiquity, their remains and fossils being found to a large extent in the coal measures, showing that ages ago Ferns grew in this country in luxuriant profusion, and not only in immense numbers but also of enormous size. As the climate of the British Isles has changed, so has its vegetation, and it is necessary now to go to tropical countries to see such Ferns as once flourished here.

It must not be forgotten, however, that the Ferns of our own time and country are of such variety and beauty of form that they will compare favourably with the more tender exotics. Indeed, comparatively few people are aware of the rich profusion of variety there is among British Ferns, all of which may be cultivated with the greatest ease and the most pleasing results.

Section 1.

GEOGRAPHICAL DISTRIBUTION OF FERNS.

FERNS have a wide geographical distribution, and are found in almost every part of the world. One thing, however, is very noticeable—it is that while these plants are found sparingly in some localities, they abound in the greatest profusion in others. There, covering the ground, clothing the mountain sides, creeping up the tree stems, hanging in festoons from the branches, they literally swarm on every side. The cause for this is the combination of warmth, moisture, shade, and shelter. Under such conditions Ferns and their near relatives, Selaginellas, revel.

Here, then, there is an indication of the condition to be copied by cultivators, that such species as are not natives of our own country may be successfully cultivated, and may present to their loving admirers some of the beauty and grace pertaining to them in their natural homes, where few are privileged to see them.

There is probably no other order of plants which has so wide a distribution, and such varied positions and habits of growth. They range from the Tropics, where they are found in greatest profusion, to the Arctic regions, as far north as Greenland. They are found at the sea-level, and up to an altitude of 16,000ft. Some grow only in hot climates, others only in cold; some in dense shade, others in full exposure to the scorching sun. They are found in damp, shady glens, gullies, forests, on mountain sides, in crevices of rocks, in old walls, bridges, and buildings, where it would appear impossible for moisture to penetrate, and where apparently there is no food for the roots to absorb. They flourish on the banks of streams, and in boggy ground; they creep over rocks, up tree stems, along the branches, clothing the trees as completely as ivy often does in this country. Some are so small that their fronds are only about half an inch in length; others are from 15ft. to 20ft. Some have stems, and grow like trees to a height of 40ft. to 50ft. Others have slender wire-like fronds, which grow many yards in length, twining round other plants, and climbing to the tops of tall trees. Indeed, among Ferns, there is every conceivable kind of growth; they grow in all sorts of places, differing entirely in their habits and requirements. Yet, with all this natural diversity, there are no other plants so easily managed.

While it is necessary to have a knowledge of the requirements of each kind in order to attain the highest degree of perfection in their cultivation, and while even with this there may be found now and again a difficult subject to manage, yet the whole family can be satisfactorily cultivated by attention to a few general rules.

RULES FOR FERN CULTURE.

These may be summarised thus: The right kind of soil must be provided; the plants must be potted or planted in a proper manner; they must be watered carefully; they must be kept at a certain temperature during winter and summer, according to that of the places of which they are natives; they should have a moist, quiet atmosphere, free from either cold draughts or currents of hot dry air; and they must have sufficient light at all times, with protection from scorching sun during summer

This may appear a formidable array of requirements, but it is surprising how easily they may be supplied; besides, the Ferns are usually so accommodating that if they do not get all they want they make the best of that with which they are supplied, and therefore no one need be afraid of attempting their cultivation. It is a most fascinating occupation, and those who begin with a few of the hardier and more easily-managed kinds invariably go on step by step until they become proficient in the management of even the most fastidious variety. Beginning with the common species, their love increases, and they do not rest until possessed of the most highly-valued members of the family.

MODES OF GROWTH.

In order to understand thoroughly the why and the wherefore of various matters, it will be well to consider first the modes of growth of different species.

Most tropical Ferns are evergreen. The fronds of one season are retained until others are produced the following season, and in some instances fronds remain green on the plants for a number of years. There are a few tropical species which are deciduous—that is, they lose their foliage at a given time, and remain without for a longer or shorter period—but it is among the species of colder climates that the deciduous kinds are most numerous. These, during their period of rest, must not be neglected. It is sometimes thought, by inexperienced cultivators, that when Ferns have lost their foliage they may be put on one side and left without water for weeks. Thus they become dust dry, the roots are injured if not killed outright, and the plants cannot possibly make the vigorous growth the following season that they would if they had been kept continually damp. Those which have lost their foliage should be supplied with water enough to keep them always moist. This will be referred to again under another heading.

The deciduous species are not quite so generally appreciated as those which are evergreen, but it must be said for them that when their new growth does appear it is often exceptionally beautiful, and possesses a freshness specially noticeable in their case. All Ferns consist of three distinct parts, viz., roots, stem, and foliage.

ROOTS.

It may seem unnecessary to many to draw attention to this fact, but among those who have not given much thought to the matter the roots and the stems are often confused. It is not necessary to say much about the roots, but it is essential that it should be clearly understood what is meant when roots are mentioned in the

ASPLENIUM SEPTENTRIONALE.
(Showing fibrous roots, stem, and fronds.)

pages of this book. They are the thin, wiry-looking fibres produced from the stem which hold the plant in its place, whether in the soil, on rocks, trees, or elsewhere, and they are also the food-seekers of the plant.

They spread about, creeping into crannies and chinks, their peculiarly-pointed tips inserting themselves in the interstices of the soil, rocks, bark of trees, or wherever they may be growing. By means of numerous fine, hair-

TREE FERN.
(Showing elongated upright caudex.)

like organs with mouths they take up moisture and other elements within their reach which are suitable food for them. The crude matter thus taken up passes in the form of sap through the stems and into the foliage, where, being acted upon by the light, it is digested and prepared for assimilation by the plant. A consideration of this fact will help the most unlearned to realise how important good healthy roots are to a plant to enable it to thrive.

STEMS.

Stems are of various characters, specified by the names caudex, rhizome, and stolon or sarmentum. Most

DAVALLIA ALPINA.
(Showing creeping rhizones.)

people who know anything about these plants are acquainted with the "Lady Fern," and the "Male Fern," so common in Britian. The foliage springs from a central crown. This crown is the top of the caudex or stem, which slowly increases in thickness and length year by year. In these Ferns the stems are of upright growth, and occasionally rise above the ground a few inches. Other species—Lomaria gibba, for instance—attain a height of 2ft. or more, producing at the top a head of spreading fronds. These are miniature tree-ferns, but Dicksonias, Alsophilas, Cyatheas, and other genera, frequently rise to a height of 50ft., producing immense heads of fronds, 20ft. to 30ft. across. These are gigantic specimens—veritable Tree-ferns. (See illustration, page 13.)

Some species have a creeping, sideways habit of growth, and thus slowly they change their position;

DAVALLIA HETEROPHYLLA.
(Showing creeping rhizomes.)

but they still belong to the section whose stems are each styled a caudex.

The next division may be represented by the "Squirrel's Foot," or "Hare's Foot" Ferns. These belong to the genus Davallia. The "feet," as they are commonly called, are often taken to be roots. This, however, is a mistake; they are not roots, but stems, botanically known as rhizomes. They correspond to the stem of the Tree-ferns, so conspicuous in their majestic height. The roots are produced underneath these creeping stems, and the fronds from their sides or tops. By these stems the Ferns travel over large spaces, spreading in all directions, and producing large quantities of foliage. Not only do they creep over the level ground, but over stones, up moist rocks, stems and branches of trees; and thus they completely clothe with their beautiful foliage spaces which might otherwise be blank and unsightly. The rhizomes of some species of Hymenophyllum are like thin black thread, delicate and easily injured. The rhizomes of others, such as the Gleichenias, are thicker, stronger, and very wiry, spreading in their native homes to such an extent that they cover acres of ground. Others are much thicker and slower in growth, their peculiar appearance giving rise to many common names, as, for instance, the "Bear's Paw" Fern (Aglaomorpha Meyeniana). The rhizomes of this species are covered thickly by a light brown, woolly-looking substance. When they divide into three or four side growths, their appearance warrants the application of the common name.

These creeping stems are not all above ground; some species produce them underground, often like dark-coloured twine, as in the Oak Fern (Polypodium dryopteris), and the Beech Fern (P. phegopteris). They work their way along, creeping between stones and other obstructions, and send up their delicate-looking foliage in profusion. These underground stems produce roots below and fronds above, just as those do which are above ground. If the growing points of these stems are broken off or injured, the growth is at once checked, and some kinds are a long time before they make a fresh start. The importance of preserving these vital parts from injury will be more fully understood when the subject of propagation has been considered.

There is another kind of stem called a sarmentum or stolon, which is produced from the caudex of certain species. The Nephrolepis are conspicuous examples of this mode of growth. From the plant rooted in a particular spot, numbers of this cord-like growth are produced, and spread to an amazing extent. They send out roots like the rhizomes already noticed, and these take hold of any damp surface with which they come in contact. Here and there a bud is formed. This soon develops into a plant, and is prepared to take up an independent existence, while the sarmentum is rambling about seeking for fresh space of which to take possession.

ASPLENIUM PRÆMORSUM LACERATUM.
(Showing frond of Fern.)

The buds formed on these stems provide a ready means of propagation, and they may be used to any extent without interference with the parent plant.

B

FRONDS OF FERNS.

The fronds are what many people call leaves. It is not necessary to enter into an explanation of the difference between a leaf and a frond, as whichever term is used it is understood to refer to the foliage. The fronds in most cases have two functions to perform—one the exposure to the light of the materials taken up the roots, whereby

ASPLENIUM VIVIPARUM.
(Showing bulbils on fronds.)

it is prepared and fitted for assimilation by the plant, and which is afterwards changed into frond, stem, or root; the other is the production of spores, commonly called seeds, for the perpetuation of its kind. In addition to spores some fronds bear upon their upper surface numbers of tiny bulbils, which develop into plants much more quickly than spores do. Ferns also breathe through their fronds as trees do through their leaves, so that cutting off fronds injures them, just as human beings are injured when by disease their lungs and digestive organs are unable to perform their functions. From these causes weakness, and eventually death, ensues. A recognition of this fact will enable many to understand why their

OSMUNDA CLAYTONIANA.
(Showing fertile and barren fronds.)

plants become sickly and die. Every time a green healthy frond is cut from a plant a direct injury is done to it, and although the effect may for a time be unnoticeable, yet if the practice be persisted in, the evil results become very conspicuous. This will suggest to the minds of Fern lovers that they must be judicious in the use of the knife if they wish their favourites to continue in a healthy condition.

In some species the sterile and fertile fronds are entirely distinct from each other, having so different an appearance that they do not appear to belong to the same plant. In the majority the fronds do not differ, the spores being produced on the under surface of the fronds without affecting their form.

ASPLENIUM AUSTRALASICUM.
(Showing undivided fronds.)

In the foliage of Ferns there is the most wonderful diversity of texture, size, and colour. Some species produce fronds little more than half an inch long—thick, fleshy, and undivided—an example being Drymoglossum piloselloides; others, as in the case of some Tree-ferns, have a length of frond 15ft. to 20ft., and a width of 10ft. to 12ft., branched again and again, divided and subdivided into countless pinnules or leaflets. Some fronds are strong, thick, and leathery in substance; others are thin and membranaceous, semi-transparent, and delicate. In some species they are undivided, as those of the Asplenium (Neottopteris) Australasicum, which attain a height of 5ft. or 6ft. and 1ft. in width; while others, as those of Todea superba and Adiantum gracillimum, are divided into minute segments, or leaflets, of exquisite beauty.

ADIANTUM GRACILLIMUM.
(Showing minute subdivision of fronds.)

Fern fronds are also of the most varied shades of colour. They range from the palest to the deepest green. Some are beautifully variegated with white, yellowish green, or red. Several have three colours in their fronds, Pteris tricolor being an example, having deep red midribs, bordered by white, with splashes of red merging into green. But it is in the young fronds of many species that the most lovely variation is seen. Some are produced a deep crimson, which gradually changes to pale green, one plant bearing several fronds, all of different shades, at the same time. Others are produced

PTERIS ARGYREA.
(Showing variegation of fronds.)

bright red, others deep pink, light pink, rose, ruby, deep brown, pale brown, and other delicate and delightful tints. Some are almost blue, being covered from foot to tip by a remarkable glaucous bloom, others are bronzy green, while several of the Selaginellas are metallic blue, S. Willdenovii having the most remarkable iridescent tints. There are also the wonderful Gold and Silver Ferns, their fronds thickly coated with bright or pale yellow, and white or cream coloured farinose powder, all giving variety in colour of foliage such as is rarely, if ever, found in other plants.

GYMNOGRAMMA OCHRACEA.
(Showing powder on fronds.)

The arrangement of the clusters of spore cases on the fronds, the remarkable diversity of the venation or veining, and other characteristics of the foliage, present a large field for study and an unending source of interest and pleasure.

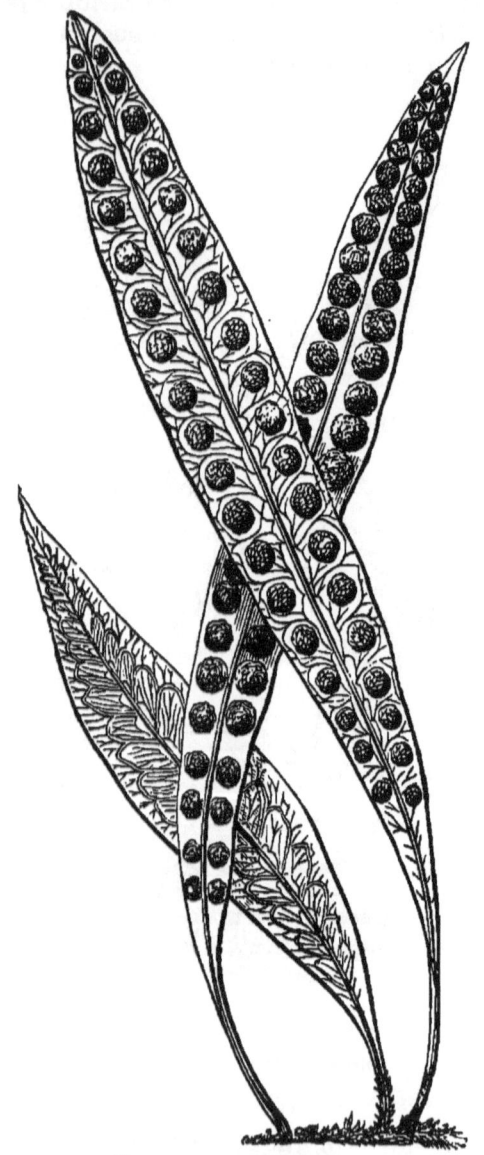

PHLEBODIUM VENOSUM.
(Showing venation and clusters of spore cases.)

Section 2.

COMPOST.

FROM the foregoing remarks it will be readily understood that Ferns grow in many different kinds of soil, and in different positions. Some species grow luxuriantly in soil of one description, and will scarcely grow at all in other kinds. It is therefore of importance to their wellbeing that they be planted in that most congenial to them. The principal ingredients required for the preparation of suitable compost are fibrous loam, leaf mould, peat, and sand. Other materials of benefit to certain kinds are sandstone, charcoal, and moss.

LOAM.

Loam is of various kinds and qualities. That with which most people are acquainted is the common garden soil, which is harsh and destitute of those qualities necessary for the wellbeing of plant life. Good loam is rich, greasy-looking, and full of body. The best type is that found in old pasture fields which have lain uncultivated year after year, and been overflowed occasionally by some stream bringing with it and depositing upon the land a rich sediment. Some loam is dark brown, some red, some yellow. Perhaps, of the three, the yellow, such as is found in Kent, is the best, but the dark brown is also excellent.

Fibrous loam is that which has more or less fibrous roots in it. The more there is the better for the plants, as, when dead, these fibrous parts consist of vegetable matter of great value to living plants. To obtain it, grass sods should be taken from a field, stacked up grass side down, layer upon layer, and allowed to remain so for a few months. It will then be found that the grass and the roots are dead. It should be chopped sufficiently small for potting purposes, and it will form the basis of a grand compost for Ferns. When the sods are cut from the field, they should be only so thick as to include the roots, three or four inches being the depth of soil to be taken from the surface; thus a mass of fibre is secured without the looser material into which the roots had not penetrated, and which, though often good, is not nearly so valuable as the fibrous part. Any stray living roots found in the loam when about to be used should, of course, be thrown out. Whenever loam is mentioned in this treatise, the term applies to the kind here described.

LEAF MOULD.

Leaf mould, or leaf soil, consists of decayed leaves. In woods and plantations, when the leaves fall from the trees in autumn, they are often blown into hollow places or ditches. There they gradually decay and form a rich, light, spongy mass of mould, containing the very elements in which Ferns revel. This is a natural production of the highest value. The best is that made up of oak and beech leaves. These should be obtained if possible; if unprocurable, then any other kind may be substituted. In places where the fallen leaves have been left undisturbed for a long time, this rich mould may be found of considerable depth. The number of fibrous roots and plants growing in this deposit testifies plainly to its value. Those who are not in the vicinity of woods, where leaves have accumulated naturally, may provide a supply by having the leaves in their gardens or along the sides of the roads and lanes, collected and placed in a heap in some out-of-the-way corner, where, exposed to the weather, they will decay, and in the course of a year or less will be sufficiently decomposed for use. The leaves, when collected, should either be in an enclosure, or have some branches placed over them to prevent their being blown about. All sticks, pieces of wood, and other foreign substances, should be thrown out, and the leaf soil kept pure.

PEAT.

At one time peat was considered to be the one necessary and all-sufficient material for Ferns, but observation and experience are convincing many that it is not of such paramount importance. The value of leaf mould is now generally acknowledged, for most species will grow equally well in it, and in some cases better than in peat. On the other hand, it must be conceded that some species are naturally bog or marsh plants, and these should have a special supply of peat.

There are different qualities of peat. The common bog found in many parts will do for Ferns planted out of doors, but for those indoors, whether in pots or rockwork, the peat should be of a different kind. That already mentioned is almost entirely decayed moss, with very little fibre if any. The best is that commonly known as orchid peat, containing sand, fibre, and fern roots. This, while it will hold moisture, also contains nutritive matter not found in the other, neither is it of so spongy a nature, but is more solid, has more substance, and is admirable as a constituent in fern compost. It is found in the South of England, especially in Kent and Hampshire, though here and there in the more northern parts of the country a good quality is also obtainable.

SAND.

The coarse silver sand found in Bedfordshire is the best; it is clean, sharp, and serves the purpose intended better than any other. Sand is used to keep the compost open, and to facilitate the passage of all surplus water through the soil. Silver sand, although the best, is not indispensable. Any clean, sharp sand will do as an inferior substitute. Clean, coarse, river sand is very good, and for the more robust free-growing Ferns suitable sand may often be procured at building excavations. If not sufficiently clean and sharp it may be washed, and when dry it will be much improved.

SANDSTONE.

This is of two kinds, the red and the white. Of the two, white is preferable for mixing with the compost for Filmy Ferns, some of the Cheilanthes, Nothoclœnas, and Pellæas. It must be broken into small pieces, and if made very small it may be used instead of ordinary sand, if there is difficulty in procuring that material.

CHARCOAL.

For certain Ferns this is very valuable. It should be broken small and mixed with that compost, which has to be kept very open and porous for the ready escape of surplus water.

MOSS.

Sphagnum moss grows in wet places, and no doubt to a large extent forms common bog. When alive and in a growing condition it is much used for orchid culture. It may be chopped small and mixed with some kinds of fern compost.

Wood moss is found in large flakes. It is useful for lining baskets, wire netting for walls, cylinders, &c., and it is also serviceable for putting over the drainage of pots, to prevent the soil washing down and stopping up the outlet.

CROCKS.

These are broken plant pots used for drainage. They must be of various sizes, according to the pots for which they are required. Bricks broken small, rough cinders, or pieces of charcoal, will answer the same purpose. There is also a patent crock now manufactured, which is handy, takes up little room, and appears to answer its purpose well.

POTTING STICKS.

These may be mentioned as accessories to the potting materials. Their use is to facilitate the pressing of the new soil regularly and firmly round the old ball of a plant when being re-potted. For example, when a plant from a 6in. pot is being put into a 7in. or 8in., without one of these sticks there would be difficulty in getting the new soil all round the ball in a proper manner. By means of the stick there is no difficulty whatever.

One stick should be 14in. or 15in. long, 1in. wide, and 1in. thick, rounded at the bottom, and the rough edges smoothed; another should be 10in. or 12in long, 1in. wide and ½in. thick; and one 8in. or 9in. long, ½in. wide, and ¼in. thick, made slightly thinner at the bottom for small pots. When these are used the potting is better performed, and there is no risk of breaking the roots. A piece of slater's lath will do for the largest, a double thick plasterer's lath for the medium, and an ordinary lath for the smallest. They should be smoothed at the top, so that they may be handled with comfort.

Section 3.

COMPOST FOR VARIOUS GENERA,
Growing in Pots, Pans, or Baskets.

BOTRYCHIUM.   OPHIOGLOSSUM.

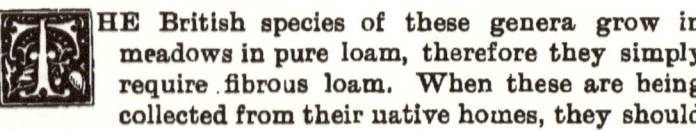HE British species of these genera grow in meadows in pure loam, therefore they simply require fibrous loam. When these are being collected from their native homes, they should be taken up with a piece of the grass sod in which they are growing, as they are difficult to establish if their roots are disturbed. The exotic species should be potted in equal parts of loam and peat.

ADIANTUM.

Fibrous loam, leaf mould, and sand, in equal quantities. Adiantum Farleyense frequently fails to grow satisfactorily, owing to having peat in its compost. Some of the strong-growing species may do with a little, but all are better without it. .

ADIANTOPSIS.	ANEMIDICTYON.
AGLAOMORPHA.	ANGIOPTERIS.
ALEURITOPTERIS.	ARTHROPTERIS.
ALSOPHILA.	ASPIDIUM.
ANEMIA.	ATHYRIUM.

BALANTIUM.
BLECHNUM.
BRAINEA.
CAMPYLONEURUM.
CERATODACTYLIS.
CETERACH (Exotic.)
CIBOTIUM.
CYATHEA.
CYRTOMIUM.
DENNSTÆDTIA.
DICKSONIA.
DICTYOGRAMMA.
DISPHENIA.
DOODIA.
DORYOPTERIS.
ELAPHOGLOSSUM.
FADYENIA.
GONIOPTERIS.
GYMNOGRAMMA.
GYMNOPTERIS.
HEMIONITIS.
HEMITELIA.
HYMENODIUM.
HYPODERIS.
HYPOLEPIS.
LASTREA.
LEPICYSTIS.
LOMARIA.
LOMARIOPSIS.
LINDSAYA.
LONCHITIS.
LITOBROCHIA.
LLAVEA.
LYGODICTYON.
LYGODIUM.
MENISCIUM.
MICROSORUM.
MOHRIA.
NEPHRODIUM.
OLFERSIA.
ONOCLEA.
PHEGOPTERIS.
PHLEBODIUM.
PHYMATODES.
PLATYLOMA.
PLEOONEMIA.
PLEOPELTIS.
PLEURIDIUM.
PŒCILOPTERIS.
POLYBOTRYA.
POLYSTICHUM.
PTERIS.
SADLERIA.
SALPICHLŒNA.
SELLIGUEA.
STENOSEMIA.
STRUTHIOPTERIS.
TRICHIOCARPA.
WOODWARDIA.

These all do well in loam, leaf mould, peat, and sand equal parts.

DRYNARIA.
PLATYCERIUM.
POLYPODIUM.
SELAGINELLA.

Loam and sand equal with half as much more leaf mould and a little chopped sphagnum moss.

ACROPHORUS.	LOPHOLEPIS.
ACROSTICHUM.	LEUCOSTEGIA.
ACTINIOPTERIS.	MARATTIA.
ANAPELTIS.	NEOTTOPTERIS.
ASPLENIUM (Exotic).	NIPHOBOLUS.
CALLIPTERIS.	NIPHOPSIS.
CAMPTOSORUS.	OLEANDRA.
DIDYMOCHLŒNA.	ONYCHIUM.
DIPLAZIUM.	OSMUNDA.
DRYMOGLOSSUM.	RHIPIDOPTERIS.
GONIOPHLEBIUM.	STENOCHLŒNA.
THYRSOPTERIS.	

For the above, loam, leaf mould, and sand in equal parts, with a double quantity of peat.

DAVALLIA.	HUMATA.
GLEICHENIA.	NEPHROLEPIS.

The same compost as the preceding, but coarser and more lumpy.

ASPLENIUM (British).	CYSTOPTERIS.
CETERACH (British).	SCOLOPENDRIUM.

Loam, leaf mould, sand, in equal quantities, with half as much old mortar, and for Scolopendriums some oyster shells broken small.

ALLOSORUS (Parsley Fern).   WOODSIA.

Equal quantities of loam, sand, and leaf mould, with a small quantity of slaty shale or broken sandstone.

CHEILANTHES.   NOTHOCHLŒNA.   PELLÆA.

Loam, leaf mould, sand, and peat in equal quantities with a little small charcoal and sandstone.

HYMENOPHYLLUM.   TODEA.   TRICHOMANES.

Loam, leaf mould, sand, and peat in equal quantities, with half as much charcoal and sandstone, all very rough and open in order to allow a free passage of water. A little chopped sphagnum moss may also be added.

Although manure is not necessary for Ferns, many do not object to it; the strong growing kinds particularly appear to like it. That from an old mushroom bed may be mixed in moderate proportion with the compost. A small quantity of Ichthemic guano, or a little powdered cow manure, may be added, but with caution.

The foregoing arrangement will be a guide to those anxious to have their plants in the best possible condition. If the arrangement is adhered to, other conditions being also favourable, the results will be entirely satisfactory.

WARDIAN CASES.

The compost for Wardian cases should consist of loam, leaf mould, sand, and peat in equal proportions, with half as much charcoal, and if for Filmies, a little broken sandstone, all rather rough and open.

WALLS. POCKETS.

Compost for Ferns planted against wired walls should be rougher than that in pots and pans, but of the same ingredients. For small receptacles like cork pockets and fern tiles fastened against walls it should be similar to that used for pots. Whenever good peat is unobtainable an extra quantity of leaf mould should be put in the compost.

ROCKWORK.

Compost for this, whether indoors or out, should be specially rough and open, the roughest being used for the bottom and the finer for the upper portion of the pockets in which the Ferns are planted. Compost for outside ferneries should consist of loam, leaf mould, sand, and peat in equal quantities, giving to Polypodiums a little extra leaf mould; to Osmundas, extra peat; to Scolopendriums a little old mortar or oyster shells crushed small. Blechnums cannot do with lime in any form. They should therefore be planted quite apart from Scolopendriums and others of similar tastes.

C

Section 4.

VARIOUS HABITS OF FERNS.

FERNS are so diverse in their habits of growth and in the character of their foliage that a knowledge of the particulars in relation to the more distinct kinds will materially assist the cultivator in providing the conditions under which the plants will be most at home.

The majority grow on the ground, on raised banks, in gullies, glens, ravines, in forests, woods, and some in the open country exposed to the full sun. These have usually upright foliage of a more or less drooping habit. They are suitable for pot culture or for planting in rockwork. Others grow in elevated positions, on the ledges of rocks, on trees, and in places where their pendent fronds hang unobstructed. These are suitable for cultivation in baskets suspended from the roof of the fernery. If in pots they should be raised up sufficiently to allow the foliage to develop naturally and show to advantage. Among these the following may be enumerated: Adiantum dolabriforme, A. caudatum, A. ciliatum, Asplenium longissimum, most of the Davallias, Goniophlebium chnoodes, G. subauriculatum, G. verrucosum, most of the Nephrolepis, Platyceriums, and Woodwardia radicans.

Others creep along the ground, over damp rocks, up the stems of trees, round and round the branches, and in every conceivable position of growth. These are suitable for planting on blocks of virgin cork for suspending, at the foot of Tree-ferns, on rockwork, or in other positions where they may freely ramble about. Members of the following genera belong to this class: Anapeltis, the smaller species of Davallia, Drynaria pustulata, Hypolepis amaurorachsis, H. distans, Niphobolus, Niphopsis, Oleandra, Phlebodium venosum, Pleopeltis, the smaller species of Polypodium, Stenochlœna, and some of the Selaginellas

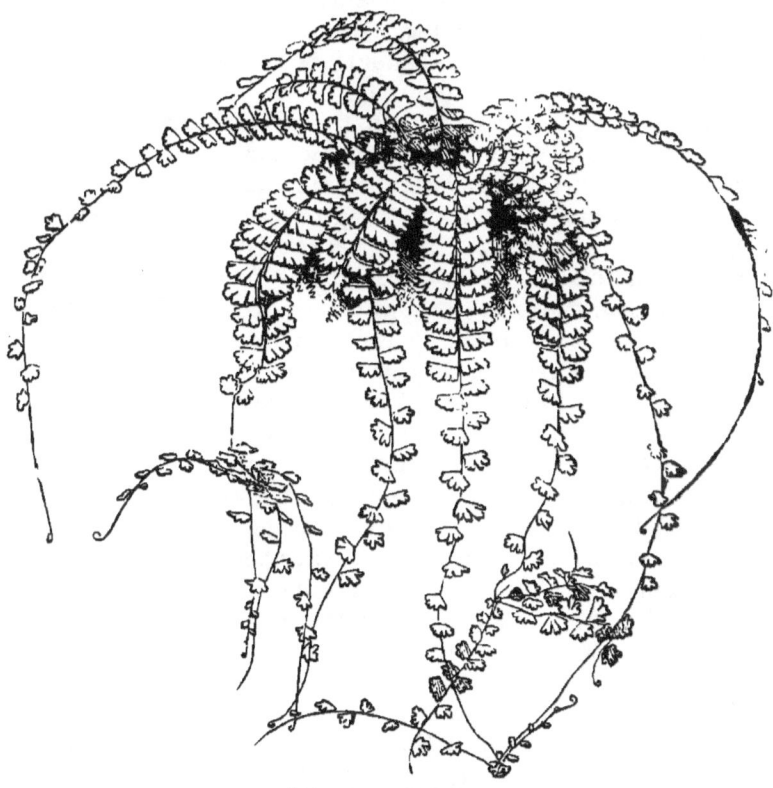

ADIANTUM CILIATUM.
(Showing pendent fronds and drooping habit.)

Most of the Cheilanthes, Nothochlœnas, and Pellæas grow in crevices of the rocks fully exposed to the weather, unless they happen to be protected by some overhanging projection. Their roots go deeply into the cracks and fissures, obtaining moisture and nutriment, while their foliage is exposed to the elements. These should be placed in light, airy positions, many of them in cool houses, just protected during winter from the frost. They must be attended to carefully, so that they may not suffer from lack of water, as their compost, being very porous, will allow the water to escape quickly. In summer they will require an abundant supply, but in winter only enough to keep them just damp.

The British Aspleniums, Ceterach and Cystopteris, have the same habits, and should be treated in like manner when cultivated in pots.

Lygodiums, Lygodictyon and Salpichlœna volubilis are climbers. They usually grow among bushes and trees, producing fronds many yards in length, taking hold of and climbing round any twig or branch with which they come in contact. They soon produce great tangled masses of foliage, while some of the fronds, taking an upward course, reach the tops of the trees. Most of the species form buds in the axils of the branches and at the apices of the fronds. From these fresh growth takes place the following year. As this is repeated again and again the fronds attain an indefinite length. This habit of growth necessitates support for the foliage. They may be trained up sticks or twine in pyramidal form; on wire netting in the shape of a cylinder three or four feet high, and the width in proportion to the size of the pot in which the plant is growing; on wire balloons; up perpendicular wires leading to the roof, and then horizontally along other wires. If planted at the base of pillars or of wire archways they may be trained so as to form a beautiful verdant covering; and if in a border, with stakes driven into the ground and wires stretched to the roofs, they may be employed to hide many an unsightly wall.

Filmy Ferns, consisting of the genera Hymenophyllum, Trichomanes, and Todea (excepting one or two of the latter), are a most beautiful and interesting section. Their fronds are thin and membranaceous in substance. Their peculiarly delicate nature necessitates their being constantly in a moisture-laden atmosphere. They are found in both tropical and temperate climates, but always in positions where it is cool, shaded, and damp.

In the warmer climates they abound in moist forests on the mountains, covering the damp rocks and clothing the stems of trees. The heavy rain and mist cause their foliage to be in a continually dripping condition, the moisture hanging in drops at the tips of the divisions of the fronds, like myriads of diamonds. In the cooler climates they grow in ravines and gullies and on dripping rocks, rarely in exposed situations.

TRICHOMANES RENIFORME.
(The New Zealand Kidney Fern.)

To imitate these conditions of growth they require a cool house, shaded from the rays of the sun, and either glazed very tightly so as to keep the house close and free from draughts, or the Ferns must be covered by glass shades or frames. Many of the species, notably the Todeas, are so hardy that they will bear many degrees of frost without injury, although it is unquestionably better to keep the temperature from falling below 35°. The Todeas have upright stems, and in time form miniature Tree-ferns. They may be planted in pots, pans, or rockwork. The Hymenophyllæ and Trichomanes are nearly all creepers. Their thin rhizomes spread freely, and necessitate their being in pans, or rockwork, or on the stems of Tree-ferns. For Wardian cases these are unequalled by any other class of plants.

HYMENOPHYLLUM TUNBRIDGENSE.
(The Tunbridge Filmy Fern.)

If the atmosphere of the house or frame can be densely laden with moisture, so as to keep the foliage always damp, the Filmies will not require watering overhead. This may sometimes be accomplished by sprinkling plenty of water on the paths, walls, stages, and rockwork. If this is not sufficient they will require dewing overhead with the fine rose of a syringe. Sometimes this causes discolouration of the foliage. When it does it is probably the result of some injurious element in the water. Only soft, tepid water should be used, and with just sufficient frequency to keep the foliage always damp.

Tree-ferns are very tropical-looking, and so distinct that specimens should be in every collection. The Alsophilas, Cibotiums, Cyatheas, Dicksonias, and some Lomarias are comparatively hardy and easily managed. The stems should be frequently syringed or watered to keep them damp. They produce many roots from the bases of the fronds at the top of the stems, and when the stems are kept damp these roots work their way down to the soil, adding thickness to the stems and strength to the plant. If a thin layer of sphagnum moss be bound round the stems with fine copper wire, it will retain the moisture and preserve the roots in their downward course; besides, many seedling Ferns will come up on it, adding much to the appearance of the tree. If the smaller species of Davallias, such as bullata, dissecta, decora, Mariesii, also Anapeltis nitida, Drynaria pustulata, and other creeping Ferns, are planted at the base of each stem, they will creep up and clothe it with foliage in a very interesting manner. Brainea insignis, Lomaria gibba, and the miniature L. L'Herminierii, with some of the Alsophilas and other genera, should have a warm greenhouse temperature, or they will not grow satisfactorily.

The Gold and Silver Ferns are not only interesting but exceedingly beautiful. The bright yellow, silvery white, or cream coloured, farinose powder more or less coating their fronds above and below, gives them a specially-attractive appearance. They are found in various climates, hence some require stove temperature, others warm greenhouse, while a few will do nicely in cool houses with a winter temperature of 35° to 40°. They belong to the genera Adiantum, Cheilanthes, Gymnogramma, Nothochloena, and Pellæa. The tropical or stove species require a dry atmosphere, so if there is any part of the house dryer than another they should be placed there. They should have an abundance of light, their roots should never be allowed to become dry, and their foliage must never be wet, either by syringing, watering, or drip from the roof.

All require the same treatment in respect to damp roots and dry foliage. If the fronds are wet by any means, the water washes off the powder, causing an unsightly appearance on the soil, and, worse still, decay of the fronds, which, of course, injures the plants.

Elk's Horn and Stag's Horn Ferns belong to the genus Platycerium, and are the most remarkable of the whole

GYMNOGRAMMA PERUVIANA ARGYROPHYLLA.
(A Silver Fern.)

family. They have received their common appellation on account of their striking resemblance to the antlers of the animals whose names they bear.

They grow upon trees, in the forks of the branches or on the stems, to which they attach themselves by their roots. The sterile fronds or shields, as they are commonly called, grow upwards, at the same time turning backwards and wrapping round the roots and body of the plant. It looks then almost like a large, green, open fan, the horizontal parts turned completely back, the other parts more or less erect and deeply lobed. The fertile fronds of some species are also erect, but entirely differentin form from the sterile. At first narrow and firm, they gradually flatten, spread out, and divide into

PLATYCERIUM ALCICORNE.
(The Stag's Horn Fern.)

deeply-cut lobes, more or less drooping. In other species, such as *grande*, they are pendent; in *biforme* they hang down several feet. Their appearance is remarkable in the extreme. The best way to cultivate this genus is by fastening the plants on pieces of charred wood, blocks of virgin cork, or pieces of Tree Fern stems suspended from the roof or against a wall.

Flowering Ferns, so called, form a curious but not a large section. That which gives rise to the term is the peculiar arrangement of the spore cases. In the majority of Ferns the spore cases are produced underneath the fronds, occasionally at the edge, and in one notable in-

OSMUNDA CINNAMOMEA.
(Example of so-called "Flowering Ferns.")

stance, Polystichum anomalum, on [the top as well as underneath. In the Flowering Ferns the spikes bearing the spore cases stand erect, in some species they spring from the sterile portion of the frond, in others the fertile fronds are entirely destitute of leafy portion. The section includes Anemia, Anemidictyon, Botrychium, Ceratodactylis, Llavea, Onoclea, Osmunda, and Struthiopteris. Other genera are sometimes included in the section, but these named are the most distinct. They do not require any special treatment, and they form a feature of interest among other Ferns.

OSMUNDA REGALIS.
(Example of so-called " Flowering Ferns.")

Section 5.

VARIOUS MODES OF CULTIVATION.

ON account of the varied modes of growth the manner of cultivation has to be varied. Ferns having an upright or a slowly-creeping rootstock (stem), or those growing from a cluster of crowns, are suitable for cultivation in pots. As they usually send their roots further down than others, the depth of soil in a pot is acceptable, and necessary to hold the tall-growing species in their places.

Those with rhizomes do not usually root so deeply, but as they spread quickly, either under or above ground, they require more surface and less depth. This is obtained by using round pans. The principal genera and species of this class are: Adiantum æthiopicum, A. amabile, A. assimile, A. capillus veneris and its varieties, A. diaphanum, A. venustum; Aglaomorpha; Anapeltis; Arthropteris obliterata; Asplenium obtusilobum; Camptosorus; nearly all the Davallias; Drymoglossum; Drynaria; Gleichenia; Goniophlebium; Hymenophyllum; Leucostegia; several Litobrochia; Lomariopsis; Lopholepis; Nephrolepis; Niphobolus; Niphopsis; Oleandra; Phlebodium; Phymatodes; Pleopeltis; many Polypodiums; Rhipidopteris; Stenochlœna; Trichomanes, and nearly all Selaginellas.

For rockwork, properly constructed, nearly all Ferns are suitable, judgment being exercised in planting the different varieties in the places best adapted for them, considering their habits of growth, size, vigour, and other necessary matters.

For baskets, some kinds are specially fitted. Many with creeping rhizomes, and others which do not creep but have drooping fronds, are suitable. A list appears further on, giving the most desirable kinds for this purpose.

Blocks of cork suspended from the roof, planted with suitable kinds, are exceedingly ornamental. For various reasons they are superior to baskets, and they look a great deal more natural. Davallias, Anapeltis, and others twine round and round them, just as they grow in their native homes, appearing to find exactly the conditions in which they delight.

Unsightly walls can be covered with Ferns and made to look very attractive, if properly done and planted with suitable varieties. Walls may also be covered with virgin cork pockets, arranged so that the Ferns planted in them may almost hide the wall. Fern tiles are used for the same purpose. They are made to fasten against the wall, joined end to end, and forming a trough to hold compost. Arranged one height above another they are better for Ferns than cork pockets, because they hold more soil. Ferns do very well in them, but until the plants have made good growth, and to a considerable extent hidden the tiles, the effect is not so pleasing as when cork is used to hide the brickwork. Narrow borders under the edges of stages, with a little rock worked in, and planted with the smaller-growing varieties, will often make a great improvement in the appearance of a house.

Dead Tree-ferns, with a nice drooping Fern planted on the top, and smaller ones fastened on with a little soil and moss, wrapped round with wire to hold them in position, look very ornamental.

Upright cylinders, of various diameters, made of wire netting lined with moss, filled with compost, and secured by a stake through the centre, form a foundation upon which may be planted creeping Davallias, Anapeltis, Lomariopsis, Oleandras, Pleopeltis, Stenochlœnas, and similarly habited species. These will soon cover the foundation by their luxuriant foliage. A pillar of this kind may be utilised for the training of Selaginella Willdenovii, with its abundant and most beautiful iridescent

46 *Ferns and Fern Culture.*

foliage, and it will constitute a splendid ornament of nature.

Iron pillars, sometimes indispensable in ferneries, and yet eyesores, if surrounded by wire netting, with room left for a lining of moss and a quantity of soil, may be converted into ornaments by planting small Ferns in the

TREE FERN STEM.
(Showing Ferns planted on it.)

moss and keeping the whole damp. They will soon grow, and pay well for the little expense and trouble incurred.

POTTING.

The time for potting stove and warm greenhouse varieties is February or the beginning of March; for hardier kinds March. It is advisable to attend to this matter just as the Ferns are beginning to grow, and before their new foliage is developed. At this stage those to be divided may be operated upon with least injury or check to them; those which require their balls reducing, and those to be put into larger pots, can all be manipulated with the least risk of injury. Large plants should be examined and potted if they require it; but it is not necessary to repot such every year. It is advisable not to do so. When they actually need it they must be carefully turned out of the pots, and if the ball will admit of reducing this should be done by means of a sharp pointed stick, worked carefully among the roots, retaining them as intact as possible, and removing the old exhausted unoccupied soil in the middle of the ball. This operation will possibly allow the plant to be put back into a pot the same size as before. Under any circumstances the plant must not be put into a pot larger than actually necessary. Smaller plants should be treated in a similar way. If they can safely be reduced let it be done, and the plants put back into pots the same size, or a little larger, as may be required. Small plants, in three or four inch pots, if pot-bound, should have their roots carefully loosened, and be put into larger sizes. The following matters cannot receive too much attention:—

Ferns must not be overpotted. They must not have their roots torn away or broken off.

A plant with its roots matted together in a hard mass should not be put into a larger pot until they have been carefully loosened as much as possible.

The overpotting of plants is unquestionably the cause of the death of thousands every year, and it must be avoided. Roots that have filled the bottom of the pot and become matted among the crocks, unless they can be safely disentangled, had better be left without disturbance at all, leaving the crocks in. The roots must not be torn away to remove the crocks, or the plant will be deprived of the best part of its feeders, and will suffer accordingly. Small plants may require potting several times during the year, as, in the growing season, under favourable conditions, they make roots very quickly.

It is by far the better plan to repot several times as required, giving a slightly larger pot each time, than to put a plant out of its pot into one much larger, with the object of saving the trouble of repotting in a month or two. The first plan will result in the plant obtaining the full value from each small supply of new soil, while the latter plan—which is really overpotting—will probably cause sickness and death. The reason for this is difficult to understand, yet it is a stubborn fact; therefore, amateurs may take warning, and professional gardeners, too, for overpotting is a very common practice.

Plants require repotting less frequently the larger they become and the larger the pots are in which they are growing. This operation may be continued through spring and summer, but it is as well to cease at the end of September. After that time little growth will be made, and the adding of new soil, if it did not cause injury to the plant, would be of no use, for its properties would be washed away before the spring by the continued watering in the meantime.

Pots must be clean when used. If new, they should be dipped in water until they cease to absorb it. Those used before must be scrubbed with a brush and hot water both inside and out, then allowed to dry before being used again. Pots dirty on the outside look slovenly; if dirty inside, they are sure to cause injury to the plant when next it has to be removed. A wet or a dirty pot will cause the new soil to adhere so tenaciously that it will be impossible to turn the plant out, for repotting, without leaving behind a lot of soil and roots, and breaking up the ball, thereby causing injury. If a new pot is used without first being dipped to a sufficient degree in water, when the plant has been put in, it will quickly absorb moisture from the soil, and probably cause the plant to suffer before the evil is detected; the soil will also adhere to a new dry pot, as it will to a dirty old one, and lead to mischief in that way.

Pots become green when in use as the result of vegetation growing upon their damp surfaces. This should be removed by frequent washing with a scrubbing brush and hot water. The result will be two-fold—improved appearance and benefit to the plant by opening the pores of the pot and allowing the passage of air to the roots.

Healthy plants having filled their pots with roots may be repotted thus: From 3in. to 4½in., from 4½in. to 6in., from 6in. to 8in., from 8in. to 10in. or 11in., and from 10in. to 13in., and so on. The measurements given are those across the pot inside at the top.

The soil and the pots being ready, the latter should be crocked, that is drained, by putting a piece of broken pot, large enough to cover the hole, hollow side downwards, with a number of others over and around it to the depth of an inch or so, according to the size of the pot. On the top should be placed a layer of moss or leaves. The object of the crocks is to allow the surplus water to drain away, and the moss is to prevent the soil washing among the crocks and stopping up the drainage, which would soon cause the soil to turn sour. The plant to be repotted may be turned out by placing the left hand over the ball of the plant, turning it upside down, and giving the edge of the pot a sharp knock on the bench. The pot may then be removed with as much soil and drainage as possible without injuring or breaking off the roots. A little soil should be put in the fresh pot on the top of the moss, the plant placed upon it, pressed down, and filled all round the ball with fresh soil, making it firm, but not hard, with the potting stick. The top of the ball should be low enough to allow a good supply of water being given—for example, in a 4½in. pot it should be ½in. below the rim, the depth being increased according to the size of the pots used.

The crowns of Ferns should be kept well out of the soil, and never buried, otherwise there is danger of their rotting. Some grow with underground rhizomes, which should be buried; others have rhizomes running on the surface, and these should be fastened down with small pegs of wood or wire.

This brings to view the necessities of those species for which pans have been recommended. Like pots, they must be clean, not wet, yet not as dry as from the kiln. They should be drained, covering the holes with large crocks, and filling up an inch or more with smaller pieces. The drainage being covered with moss or some substitute, there should be put in a layer of very rough compost, higher in the middle than the sides, then some a little finer, and so on, until there is sufficient to plant the Ferns. When this is firmly done, and all the rhizomes pegged down and well watered, it will require little further attention, except watering, for some time.

As the rhizomes grow they will have a tendency to come over the side. This should be prevented by carefully turning them on to the soil and pegging them securely. The rhizomes will then continue to root and add strength to the plant; but when they get beyond the damp soil, and stretch over the side, they cease sending out roots, and instead of adding to the strength of the plant they have to be supported by it, which results sooner or later in unnecessary exhaustion.

The compost in the centre of the pan may be raised in the form of a cone, using rough pieces of peat as a foundation, all being made quite secure. This will provide greater surface, and a congenial position for the rhizomes of the smaller Davallias, Anapeltis, &c., which will creep up, over, round and round, and make specially beautiful specimens. A little extra care will be required to prevent these becoming dry.

Ferns to be repotted must not be wet and sodden, nor yet very dry. The operation cannot be performed satisfactorily in either case. The soil should just be in want of water. If too wet, it will become very hard in the process of repotting; if too dry, the water will not afterwards penetrate the old ball, it will become dust dry, and the plant is sure to suffer.

The roots should be spread out as much as possible, not crammed together in a bunch, as is sometimes done.

BASKETS.

Baskets should be made up every spring, as the large amount of water given to them during the previous season is sure to have washed away all the good qualities of the soil not absorbed by the Ferns. Baskets are to be seen in various shapes, and made of various materials—

the highly-ornamental wire basket, and the plainer kinds of galvanised wire; the square wood and the terra-cotta baskets, such as are often used for orchids.

The very ornamental ones are often difficult to deal with, and they have also a tendency to look artificial, and not in character with the plants. The plain, galvanised baskets, with stiff suspending wires, are for some reasons preferable. The wooden ones, when not too heavy, look still better and more rustic; the terra-cotta are sometimes passable, and at others objectionable.

BASKET WITH FERNS PLANTED.

Individual taste must decide the kind to be used; so far as the Ferns are concerned all are much alike to them.

The best material wherewith to line the baskets is green wood-moss, in as large thick flakes as can be procured. The next is living sphagnum. A good thick lining should be placed in large baskets, and a few large pieces of charcoal, to partially fill the basket, so that it will not be so heavy as if filled entirely by soil. Smaller baskets will require less moss and will do without charcoal. If moss is not procurable, pieces of fibrous peat may be used, but this looks clumsy compared with the other. The wood-moss, or sphagnum, if in good condition, and placed green side out, will often grow, adding materially to the appearance of the basket.

When the Ferns are planted, the centre should be lower than the sides, otherwise when water is given it will run off instead of through the soil.

There are many beautiful Ferns suitable for this style of culture, a list of which is given further on. If small Ferns and Selaginella are planted in the sides and bottom of the basket the appearance is improved.

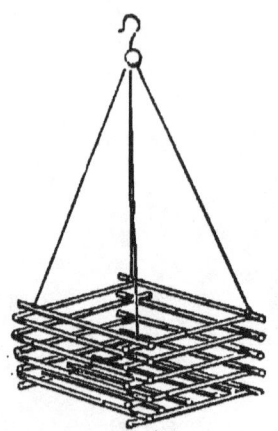

BASKET READY TO BE PLANTED.

HANGING BLOCKS OF VIRGIN CORK.

To prepare these, various sizes of slightly-curved or semi-tubular pieces should be selected; copper tacks, one inch long; thin copper wire, like thread, to secure the plants on the cork, and thicker copper wire for suspending the blocks; some large flakes of moss and ordinary open compost, such as is recommended for Davallias. The piece of cork should be laid ornamental side down; copper tacks should be driven into it just below the edges, two inches apart. One large or several pieces of moss must then be laid on the cork, green side down, a little compost put upon it, and the Ferns put in position. The whole should be pressed firmly down, the moss hanging over the sides must be turned over the soil and worked round the crowns of the plants and under the rhizomes of those of that mode of growth. A length of thin wire must be fastened to a tack at one side and carried over to a tack on the other side, giving it a turn round that, and so on backwards and forwards until the network is sufficient to hold the moss, soil, and

BLOCK OF VIRGIN CORK WITH FERN.
(For suspending.)

Ferns firmly in position. The tacks should each be driven up to the head and all will be secure. The hangers must be formed of thicker wire, pushed through the cork, turned up and knocked in to be quite firm, the tops drawn together and united by a hook, as in the case of ordinary wire baskets. All rhizomes should be pegged down on the moss, the plants watered, and the operation will be complete.

The first result obtained is a much more natural-looking mass of Ferns than can possibly be in any kind of basket—the ultimate result is a very beautiful object when the creeping Davallias and others have twined round and hidden the whole block by their lovely foliage.

For suspending from the roof three or four hangers should be attached, but if to hang against a wall one only is necessary. In the latter case the position of the plants on the cork will have to be considered, so that they may hang gracefully and to the best advantage. When, by oversight, these or baskets of other descriptions have become very dry, it is advisable to dip them in a pail of water for a few minutes. Ordinarily they may be watered in the usual way by a can with a rose.

FERNS IN ROCKWORK.

When planted in rockwork, indoors or out, Ferns require much less attention than when in pots. They do not need watering so frequently, neither do they require re-planting nearly so often; but when the compost is good and the drainage perfect they will grow for years without having to be disturbed. They attain a size and luxuriance rarely seen under other modes of cultivation. When rockwork is being planted there must be due consideration of the size to which the plants will grow; also their habits, so that overcrowding may be avoided. They must have room to develop their fronds perfectly, and the large ones must not bury or keep the light unduly from the smaller species. All should be so arranged that light may penetrate to every plant, otherwise the result will not be satisfactory.

MOSS-COVERED WALLS.

One way of hiding unsightly walls is by stretching in front lengths of wire netting of 2in. mesh. This must be secured by hooks driven into the wall of sufficient strength and number to hold the wire in position, about five inches from the wall. When the lower length is fixed it must be lined with moss, on the same principle and for the same purpose as the wire baskets. The space behind should be filled with rough open compost. The Ferns should be planted as the work proceeds, this being much more easily done than when left to the last. As one height is completed the next may be taken in hand, and so on till the whole wall is covered. Each height of wire must be fastened by its lower edge to the one below it to prevent its bulging, or the trickling out of compost. If moss is unprocurable, the lining may be of thin flat pieces of peat, filled behind in the usual way, but this does not produce so pleasing an effect.

WALLS COVERED WITH CORK.

This method requires patience and perseverance, but by its adoption walls may be made very rustic-looking. The flattest pieces of cork are most easily put on. They must be pressed close to the wall, and firmly secured by means of strong nails driven through the cork and between the bricks. The more circular pieces should be used to form pockets to hold Ferns. The pockets should be 12 or 14 inches deep, fitting close at the bottom, projecting at the top. Such pieces as cannot be pressed to the wall easily may be made more pliable by cutting a slit in the inner surface to weaken it, and to allow of its being flattened. When the wall is covered, the crevices should be filled with green moss; the holes in the pockets should also be plugged with moss or peat, to prevent the compost trickling or being washed out. All formality of arrangement should be avoided, and there should be sufficient pockets, so that when the Ferns are growing the cork will be fairly well hidden.

WALL TILES.

When these are used they must be very securely fastened, as the soil in them is very heavy when wet. They give more room for the roots than the cork pockets. After fixing them according to the instructions given by the manufacturers, they should be filled with compost to such a height that when the plants are in the surface may be an inch below the rim.

ROCKWORK (INDOORS).

It is impossible to give more than a few general directions on this subject in the space at disposal.

The construction of a rock fernery in a natural manner requires great experience, combined with a knowledge of the various requirements of Ferns.

The stone suitable for the purpose is of three kinds—sandstone, tufa, and limestone. Sometimes clinkers, or large pieces of coke dipped in thin cement, are used. These, however, are but a poor substitute for stone.

The plan of construction in all cases must depend largely upon the space at command. Where it is possible to go down into the ground the effect will be much finer than when the rockwork is all above the ground-level. The beauty of Ferns is seen to best advantage when looked down upon. The walks should undulate and wind to and fro; they should be made of stone or concrete with rugged steps here and there, the stone rising on each side, as though the whole were cut out of the solid rock. Bold projections may be arranged at intervals, and so cause an entirely new view each step that is taken. In building the stone together large pockets should be provided, to hold a good supply of compost, and these should be so arranged that they may be connected with the bulk of the soil on which the body of the rock is built. The arrangement of the stone should be irregular and free from any appearance of artificiality. The receptacles for the plants should recede as they rise, and the rock should be fixed so that the light may get to the lowest part without obstruction.

Arches may be ornamental, but they are not natural, and though to a limited degree they may be tolerated in a large place, the fernery will look better and more natural without them, and certainly the Ferns will grow more satisfactorily.

However large or small the fernery may be, it should continually be kept in mind that vegetation below the eye should be in equal or better condition than that above. This can be secured only by allowing full access of light to every plant, therefore all undue obstruction must be avoided.

The rockwork in a house must always be on a proportionate scale to the house. Too much spoils the whole—better have too little than have it overdone.

OUTDOOR FERNERIES.

There are many places in gardens where flowering plants will not live, and in some of these Ferns will grow beautifully, and convert an uninteresting spot into a source of interest and much pleasure.

But there are so many exceedingly lovely varieties of Hardy Ferns that it would be a great mistake to plant them merely to fill a vacant space. They are worthy of special attention, and of the most favourable position that can be provided for them.

Hardy Ferns are easy to manage—in fact, there are no other plants so easy of culture, and certainly none which present so large a variety of graceful habit and curious forms.

The easiest and most satisfactory mode of culture is to plant them in borders, beds, or rock ferneries.

Many Fern lovers are so placed that they have not even a small garden in which to make a fernery. When such is unfortunately the case, so unlikely a place as a back garden may be utilised. A few rough boxes, six or eight inches deep, covered with pieces of thin virgin cork, will make suitable and rustic-looking receptacles for them. The boxes should have holes bored through the bottoms, an inch or two of broken pots placed inside for drainage, next a layer of moss or leaves, and then the compost. Some of the common British Ferns planted in these contrivances will yield much pleasure and serve to add no little charm to an otherwise dreary outlook.

A Fernery on a larger scale may be made by building an edging of burrs two layers in height filled in with compost. This would prove suitable, and may be provided with little trouble and expense. Those who have gardens should select a shaded and sheltered position, as little exposed to the sun as possible, and protected from strong winds. The fernery may take the form of a border or bed. A position with a north aspect is th one most suitable, so that the plants may have a maximum of light without scorching sun.

Ferns may be planted among shrubs, but it is better to have the border or bed entirely of Ferns, so that there may be nothing to interfere with the special characteristics of these plants. There should be a mixture of proper compost put into the border, to enable the Ferns to grow satisfactorily.

The most pleasing kind of fernery is that constructed of stone in the form of rockwork. It may be on the

FERNERY ON LEVEL GROUND.

level ground, with mounds of soil and stone built up like miniature hills, with intervening valleys ; or in the form of a glen, or ravine, excavated to a greater or less depth. In either case the paths should undulate, wind in and out, and should approach in appearance as near as possible a wild rocky pathway.

An excavated fernery will present a better appearance than one on the level ground ; the vegetation and its surroundings being below the eye from various points of observation will be seen to greater advantage. Still, a very beautiful arrangement is possible without excavation.

In the construction of an outdoor fernery, as with an indoor, experience, combined with a knowledge of natural rock formation and the requirements of Fern-life, is necessary before anyone can undertake and carry

EXCAVATED FERNERY.

through successfully the building of a large rockwork fernery.

The following suggestions will help those who desire to attempt the work :—

In whatever form the fernery may be arranged, drainage should be provided for the escape of surplus moisture.

When it is a mound or ridge raised on the level ground, holes may be dug down to the sand, filled with broken bricks, clinkers, or stones covered with sods, or other rough material, and the body of soil above. This will provide a ready means for all surplus moisture to pass away. If the fernery be sunk in the ground the water will drain to the lowest part, and there provision must be made for its disposal, either by enabling it to sink

FERNERY IN FORM OF A MOUND.

into the sand below, or by constructing a drain to carry it elsewhere.

Sandstone is one of the best materials for rockwork. Its colour harmonises with the various tints of foliage, and all Ferns grow well in association with it. This stone is found in strata having a gentle dip in a given direction, therefore when it is used the natural formation should be imitated.

Limestone is hard, and found in all sorts of curious shapes. By the action of water some pieces have holes through them, others channels washed in their surface, with numerous chinks, crevices, and inequalities of outline. With this material a very ornamental rockery may be constructed, in which Ferns will grow luxuriantly and with pleasing effect.

In commencing the construction, the paths should first be planned. From these the rockwork should rise in an irregular mass. Large pockets should be formed in communication with the bulk of the soil constituting the foundation of the fernery.

The general outline should take the form of a series of terraces, rising tier above tier, receding farther and farther from the path. Blocks of stone here and there should be placed to give character to the construction, and to prevent the view being too extended from any one point.

Every stone must be made perfectly secure, so that rain, frost, and other influences may not destroy or cause injury to the erection.

When the building is complete, some good compost for the Ferns should be put into the pockets, in which to plant the Ferns. Sometimes tree roots are used, but they soon commence to decay, so they are not at all suitable for a fernery which is to be of a lasting character.

ROCK-FERNERY WITH GLASS PROTECTION.

There is a wonderful difference between the condition of Ferns growing in the open air and those cultivated in a frame or unheated greenhouse. When protected from the extremes of heat and cold, wet and drought, storms, boisterous winds, and other injurious influences, their foliage develops more perfectly, is of greater beauty, and lasts much longer in nice condition. Not only are there these advantages, but species such as Adiantum capillus veneris, Asplenium lanceolatum, A. marinum, and others, which rarely grow satisfactorily in the open air, may be successfully cultivated with the simple protection of a cold frame. When this form of fernery is being constructed, the walls should go well into the ground, the soil be excavated to the depth of 2ft., some good compost being put [in. A miniature rockery may be built with elevations, depressions, pockets, niches, and cosy corners for rare and beautiful little species.

Sandstone, limestone, or tufa may be used for the rockwork. The frame should have a northern aspect, the stone being built up inside to hide the walls, and to give the whole of the central part as diversified an arrangement as can be secured in the space.

This will form a perfect treasure-house to the Fern lover, for here, with the greatest ease, may be cultivated many dwarf kinds of various genera, which are more liable to be lost when fully exposed to the elements.

A frame should be occupied only by the smaller species—the larger and stronger would be out of place.

Built in the manner described, facing the north, abundance of light would be secured without the scorching rays of the sun. The frame should have a good elevation at the back, to give the glass at least an angle of 45°. Being sunk in the ground, the temperature would be equable during both summer and winter. In the former the heat would have little effect, and during the winter it would be largely secure from the frost. If planted in good compost the roots would revel in the cool moist position among the stones, and the foliage, being hardened by a gentle and continued circulation of air overhead, provided by tilting the lights more or less according to the weather, would be more beautiful than even in their native rocks.

By carrying out this arrangement of rockwork in an unheated house an additional benefit may be obtained, as then the cultivator can walk about, and being under cover may enjoy the pleasure attending the cultivation of his plants, whatever the weather outside may be. Being on a larger scale, larger species may be accommodated and greater variety obtained also.

The cultivation of Ferns under these conditions is as simple as it possibly could be. Once planted the only attention necessary for a long time would be the giving of water and the ventilation, while the results would be highly gratifying.

Section 6.

LIGHT.

IT is a very common idea that Ferns grow best in dense shade. This, however, is altogether erroneous. It is true that some kinds of Filmy Ferns are found growing in comparatively dark places, but Ferns generally not only can do with an abundance of light but they are much better with it.

A fernery should have in every case possible a northern aspect. A southern aspect is not good, because, unless shaded in some manner by trees or buildings, during the summer it receives the full glare of the sun, and means must then be taken to protect the plants from the strong light and scorching rays. A span-roof fernery should be built with its length running north and south, and all roofs should have a pitch of 45° or 50°. A flatter roof than this is likely to cause drip, which is as injurious to Ferns as to other plants. A lean-to fernery, with northern aspect, will require very little shading, even during summer, and not any during the greater portion of the year. The nearer the aspect is to the south, the more shading will be required.

The rule is to provide the fullest possible amount of light at all times, merely shading, when actually necessary, to prevent very strong sunlight scorching or bleaching the foliage.

From the beginning of September to the beginning of March, shading will not be required on a fernery of any aspect; on the other hand, the glass should be repeatedly washed outside and in, to enable all the light to penetrate the fernery. The accumulation of soot and dirt on the glass during winter becomes very detrimental to the wellbeing of plants if allowed to remain. Fogs are a great cause of this deposit, and not only so but the ingredients of fog deposit are much worse to remove than ordinary dirt if once allowed to become dry. It will be wise, therefore, to be lavish in the use of warm water and brush to the outside during the autumn and winter months. If the glass and rafters inside are washed occasionally with warm water and sponge the house will look cleaner and the plants will be much better for the labour expended. In the beginning of March the atmosphere becomes much clearer, the sun gains strength, and a little shade soon becomes necessary for houses containing stove Ferns if exposed fully to the sun. The hardier greenhouse kinds will not require shade for some time, and hardy Ferns not for two or three months. The position of the house and the character of its inmates will determine the time when shading becomes necessary.

MEANS OF SHADING.

Shade may be provided by blinds, or by one of numerous preparations put upon the glass. Blinds form the best means of shading. They should be fastened on rollers, and so arranged that when the rope is released the blind will roll down, and when no longer required may be rolled up again and secured in its place.

There are various kinds of material suitable for blinds. Thick Tiffany, Frigi domo, closely woven cotton netting, and "The Willesden" rot-proof scrim canvas, the latter being preferable to any of the others, as it combines shading qualities with durability. These vary in thickness. For a house greatly exposed the thicker material may be selected. Where little shade is required a thinner material will be more suitable. The great advantage connected with blinds over the permanent shading material is that on wet, dull days, when there is little or no sunshine, by keeping the blinds rolled up the full light is admitted to the plants, greatly to their advantage. Also, every day, until the sunlight becomes too strong, and in the afternoon and evening, when the sun is no longer a source of danger, the plants can have the full light. This is of the highest importance; it is the cause of health and vigour of plants, which under other conditions of shade would have been weakly and of far less beauty.

When permanent shading is used in the form of powder sold for the purpose, white should be selected; green may obscure the glass more and produce a heavier shade, but this is beneficial only for a small portion of the time it is on the glass. It keeps out too much light at other times, and even if only a thin coating is put on the colour is objectionable. Cream colour is better than green, but white is best of all, for it will allow more light to penetrate on a wet or dull day, a matter not to be despised.

Whatever colour is used, it should be put on neatly. The practice of syringing it on produces a most untidy appearance as well as imperfect shade, and should not be tolerated anywhere. As soon as it possibly can be dispensed with, all shading should be removed, and the plants allowed the unrestricted light. Ferneries should never be glazed with green glass, but always with the clearest that can be obtained.

Section 7.

TEMPERATURE.

FERNS require more or less heat, according to their natural place of growth. Most of those from the Tropics require stove temperature.
If, however, they grow high up the mountains, where the temperature is much lower than near the sea level, they may be cultivated in a warm or cool greenhouse. Some species are found in both hot and cold climates, hence they may be cultivated in various temperatures.

For convenience of cultivation the whole family may be divided into classes—those requiring stove temperature, those suitable for a warm greenhouse, and those which may be successfully cultivated in cool greenhouse; those more hardy for cold greenhouse or frame, and the perfectly hardy species.

STOVE TEMPERATURE.

This need not be so high for Ferns as is often supposed, neither must it be as high in winter as in summer. Taking December as the starting point, the night temperature should be 60° to 65°, rising to 70° during the day. About the middle of January the days lengthen, and as the light becomes stronger and of greater duration, the temperature should gradually rise and continue to do so until by the end of May the maximum is reached at 70° by night and 75° to 80° by day. This temperature should be maintained during June and July, when it should be gradually reduced, until by the end of November the lowest point is again reached, at the season when the days are short and the light faint. At any time the temperature may rise 5° or 10° higher, as the result of sun heat, but it is not wise to give more artificial heat than is necessary to maintain a temperature indicated by these figures.

WARM GREENHOUSE.

The temperature in December will be sufficiently high at 45° to 50° by night, and 50° to 60° by day. As the days increase in length the temperature should gradually rise, until by the end of May it is 60° to 65° by night, and 70° to 75° by day. In August it should begin to decline, until the lowest point is reached in November.

COOL GREENHOUSE.

In a cool greenhouse the winter temperature by night should be 40°, though 35° might not do any harm ; during the day 45° to 50° should be maintained. In spring a gradual rise should take place, until artificial heat is dispensed with for the summer. The temperature, when dependent upon natural heat, may sometimes, even in summer, be so low, owing to a continuation of wet, cold weather, that a little fire heat becomes advisable for a short time. On the other hand, there is occasionally such intensely hot weather that it becomes difficult to keep the temperature down. This may be done by extra shading, and a free use of water sprinkled on the paths, walls, and stages, or rockwork.

COLD GREENHOUSE.

The temperature of a house where there are no means of supplying artificial heat should be regulated during winter by outside covering. Perfectly Hardy Ferns are the only suitable kinds to have in a house where the frost may penetrate, and even for these it is well to use all possible precautions to keep out the frost. Hardy Ferns will bear many degrees without apparent injury, but it is certainly an advantage to them when kept above freezing point. When frost penetrates, it immediately affects everything damp. It often breaks pots, and when it is severe it hurts the roots against the sides. By covering the place with mats or other materials, the effects of the frost may be reduced considerably, and by plunging all pots in cocoa-nut fibre or leaf mould the evils may be further reduced, resulting in undoubted benefit to the plants.

VENTILATION.

Means for ventilation should always be provided. Ferns must not be subjected to cold draughts, yet a gentle imperceptible supply of fresh air given at the proper time will prove of great benefit. There must be provision for the entrance of this at the lower part of the house, and for the escape of hot air at the top.

Often there are no means provided at the bottom for the entrance of air, and when the ventilators at the top are opened, a cold current at once rushes in, causing the moisture to condense upon the foliage. In winter this is particularly injurious to the plants, chilling them and leading to discolouration of the foliage. By opening ventilators at the bottom the fresh air enters at the proper place, while the hot air freely escapes at the top. An upward current is thus produced which prevents chilly down draughts.

Ventilation may be given whenever the temperature is high enough, care being exercised not to open the ventilators so wide that the temperature is suddenly reduced. On windy or cold days special care will be necessary. Air should be given as early in the morning as possible, and left on as long in the afternoon as is safe. This conduces to a sturdy growth, the foliage being harder and more enduring than would otherwise be the case.

WATERING.

There is more importance attaching to the watering of plants than many people imagine. It must not be done in a haphazard or careless manner, for injurious watering causes a long train of evils. A clear and perfect knowledge of the proper way can be obtained only by experience, but a little care in following certain rules will enable the merest novice to steer clear of many dangers.

The soil in which Ferns are growing should always be kept damp, but not in so thoroughly a wet condition as to make it sodden. If it becomes very dry the plant droops, shrivels, and sometimes dies ; if it is always very wet it soon becomes sour.

Plants should be examined every day ; in the morning during winter, in the afternoon or evening during summer. Some plants will require water one day, others the next. Whenever a Fern is becoming dry it should be well watered, and not again until it requires it. It is a bad practice to water plants when it is not necessary ; it is also a bad plan to give only a little at a time, as by that means the surface appears damp while at the roots the soil is often dust dry. If the pot receives a sharp rap the sound will at once indicate the condition of the soil. If it be a ringing sound like that of a bell the plant should have water, if it be dull and heavy, water is not needed. If the plant does not actually require water at the usual time of watering one day, but appears likely to become dry before the ordinary time next day, it should be watered in a few hours, out of the usual course. If this is not practicable it will be better to water at once than run any risk of its suffering in the interval. The water given should be of the same temperature as the atmosphere of the house, or, at least, it should have the chill taken off.

Watering Ferns under glass by means of a hose-pipe attached to a cold water tap cannot be too strongly condemned. The water being colder than the air chills the plants, many receive water when they do not require it, and others may be missed; the foliage becomes drenched, and a state of sickness soon ensues. All Ferns, except Filmies, should have their foliage kept dry, and should neither be watered overhead nor syringed. The foliage so treated soon becomes discoloured, and dies, or it has to be removed because of its objectionable appearance. This is a direct injury to the plant.

Sometimes, to save trouble or to cause a pretty (?) effect, perforated pipes are laid round the fernery, so that by turning a tap the whole place can be filled by sprays of water. This is a thoroughly bad practice and cannot possibly end in anything but disaster.

Whether in pots, baskets, planted in rockwork, in pockets, fern-tiles, or moss-covered walls, there is no safe way of watering but by means of a can with or without a rose. It certainly involves more time and labour, but the results far more than compensate for the extra trouble. Anyone refusing to spend the necessary time and care in properly watering the plants must be content to have less satisfactory results.

When a plant in pot or basket has become very dry it should be placed in a pail of water for ten or fifteen minutes until the soil is thoroughly wet.

Some cultivators have an idea that Ferns should be "dried off" in autumn to give them a rest; even evergreen varieties are treated so, while the deciduous kinds when they have lost their foliage are put away and do not receive water for weeks. This is wrong treatment altogether. Deciduous as well as evergreen kinds should always be kept damp. They do not need water so frequently in winter as in summer, because they do not take up so much moisture from the soil, and there is not so much evaporation going on. Yet they must be watered with sufficient frequency to keep the roots always moist. Ferns growing wild in this country get a great deal more water in winter than in summer; notwithstanding this they lose their foliage and rest. Their rest is not brought about by a lack of water, but to a large extent by a lowering of the temperature. So, under glass, if the temperature is reduced, this, with the diminution of light, will bring a cessation of growth in a natural manner. When the days begin to lengthen and the temperature to rise, the plants will soon show vitality and grow vigorously after their rest.

CUTTING FERNS DOWN.

There is a common idea that Ferns should have all their foliage cut off in winter. This should not be done while the fronds are green. The dead foliage of the deciduous kinds should be removed when they are in greenhouses, as it looks unsightly, but the foliage of evergreen kinds should not be cut off until it becomes discoloured, or is in the way of the development of new foliage. In the case of such as the Maiden Hair, where the new fronds are produced very thickly together, it is wise to remove the old just as the new ones begin to appear. If left on till the new growth is pretty well advanced, there will be more difficulty in removing them, and the new fronds might be damaged. But in the case of species producing only a few fronds in a season, and those at long intervals, the old foliage should be left until it becomes unsightly. As long as a frond is green it is of benefit to the plant, and every green frond cut off is a more or less severe loss to it.

MOISTURE IN THE ATMOSPHERE.

This should always be maintained, especially during the growing season. It can best be done by sprinkling the paths, walls, and stages, or rockwork more or less freely with water. On hot dry days this will be most beneficial, not only to maintain the required dampness, but to keep down the temperature. In winter, when the fires are being pushed strongly to keep up the temperature, the artificial heat will cause a dry, parched air, which must be remedied in the manner recommended.

A dry atmosphere has not only a tendency to restrict development of foliage, but it encourages insect pests of various kinds; yet the other extreme must be avoided. Too much moisture may cause the plants to damp off, and will thus prove an evil. Judgment must be exercised in order to obtain the condition most congenial to the plants by attention to temperature, light, shade, moisture, and ventilation, avoiding excess in everything.

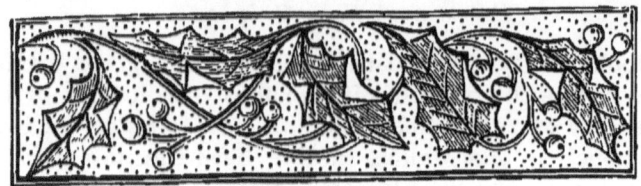

Section 8.

FERNS IN DWELLING-HOUSES.

THE condition of atmosphere and the lack of light in dwelling-houses are such that few Ferns can grow satisfactorily. They have a better chance where oil is burned than when gas is used for lighting, because gas dries and vitiates the atmosphere to a much greater extent. They have also a better chance in large than in small rooms, as the fluctuations of temperature are neither so sudden nor so extreme.

They are often killed by not having sufficient light. They are frequently placed a long distance from the window, where they soon become weak and sickly-looking, and their owners wonder whatever is the cause. It is impossible for plants to be healthy and strong without plenty of light; therefore they should be as near the window as possible, and be shaded only from the hot rays of the sun.

A north window is the best, as the light is usually allowed unrestricted entrance, neither is there any risk of scorching at a window of this aspect. They do well facing east, west, or south, though at the latter they must be shaded when necessary. Apart from this, they must have all the light with which it is possible to provide them.

They should be kept out of draughts, as cold currents of air do them harm. A hot, dry atmosphere, caused by large fires and burning of gas, is also injurious.

Water must be given in sufficient quantity, and often enough to keep them damp. They may not require a supply every day, but they should be examined every day. Ferns in small pots will require watering more frequently than those in large ones; more attention is also necessary when they are in warm than in cold rooms, and in summer than in winter.

Tepid water must always be given. They must not be allowed to stand in saucers of water, for this causes the soil to go bad, and the roots to rot. The water should be given at the top, and that which drains into the saucer must be emptied away.

When plants become dusty they should be cleaned by means of a soft sponge and warm water, or a soft brush. It is not wise to put tender Ferns outside when it rains.

When suitable varieties are procured, and attention bestowed upon them, there are no other plants so graceful and beautiful for house decoration, and none which brighten up and add so much to the cheerfulness of a room.

WARDIAN CASES AND FERN STANDS.

A large number of Ferns may be cultivated in a dwelling-house when they are planted in Wardian cases. The glass keeps off the dust, and prevents the access of impure air; it also keeps the atmosphere quiet and damp. This is a great advantage, enabling many Ferns to grow beautifully which could not possibly live if not so protected.

Fern stands usually consist of an earthenware bottom, with a glass shade fitting inside the rim. These are suitable for a small number of plants, but the Wardian cases may be made to hold any number.

The larger cases are often made with a door at each end, but a better plan is for one side to open, as this allows freer access to every part. Every stand and case must have provision for drainage and for the escape of all surplus water. The terra-cotta stands usually have a hole at the sides, which may be closed by a cork when the surplus water has escaped. The wooden cases should be lined with zinc, and have a small tap by which to draw off water drained to the bottom. A layer of broken pots, cinders, or gravel should be put at the bottom, about 1in. thick. On this should be placed moss or leaves, then very rough compost, with finer at the top. (For kind of compost see under heading "Compost for Wardian Case.")

It is well for the soil to be a little higher in the centre than at the sides; it should be pressed down moderately firmly, to prevent its sinking afterwards. (For Ferns suitable for cases see list further on.) After being planted, the Ferns should be well watered, Filmy Ferns overhead, other kinds only at the roots. Tepid water should always be given.

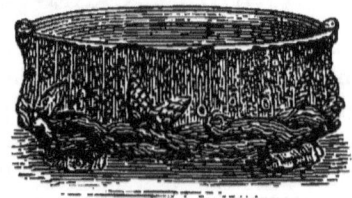

FERN STAND AND GLASS.   FERN STAND.

The case should be placed as near the window as possible. Facing north is the best aspect and facing south the worst. The Ferns must have all the light possible, but must be shaded from the hot sun. After a thorough watering, little attention will be required for some time. They should be examined every two or three weeks, and as soon as they appear to be getting dry they should be well watered. Care must be exercised not to over-water them, as fungus or mould will make its appearance, and the fronds will damp off. When too wet, a green slimy growth sometimes comes on the soil, and spreads to the

WINDOW CASES.

These are made on the principle of the window boxes, with glass all round and above, thus enclosing and protecting the plants from winds, storms, dust, and other adverse influences to which those in simple window boxes are exposed. The cases being built against the window access is obtained by lifting the sash. This may be raised the greater part of the day, but closed when necessary to prevent dust settling upon the plants; also when the room becomes hot from the burning of gas or from other cause.

During severe weather, if the sash be raised, the warmth of the room will help to keep the plants free from frost. The Ferns may either be planted in soil or kept in pots. When in the latter they will need water more frequently than when planted out, as the soil in a pot dries more quickly than a larger body filling the bottom of the case. If exposed to the sun the case must be shaded at al times when there is risk of the Ferns being scorched.

 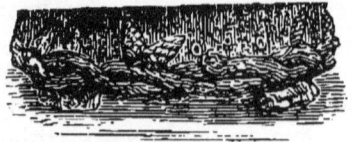

FERN STAND AND GLASS.   FERN STAND.

The case should be placed as near the window as possible. Facing north is the best aspect and facing south the worst. The Ferns must have all the light possible, but must be shaded from the hot sun. After a thorough watering, little attention will be required for some time. They should be examined every two or three weeks, and as soon as they appear to be getting dry they should be well watered. Care must be exercised not to over-water them, as fungus or mould will make its appearance, and the fronds will damp off. When too wet, a green slimy growth sometimes comes on the soil, and spreads to the

WINDOW BOXES.

Windows may be greatly improved in appearance by boxes of more or less ornamental character placed upon the sills, and filled with plants. The position of some windows is not at all suitable for flowering plants, but shade-loving Ferns would grow there very nicely. The boxes, if made of wood, should be as wide and deep as the position will allow, and be covered with virgin cork, so that the ordinary wood is entirely hidden from all points of view, inside and out. They should have holes burnt through the bottom to allow the water to drain away. They should be raised about an inch from the sill, to allow a circulation of air underneath, which will add to their durability.

A layer of crocks at the bottom, a covering of moss or leaves, and the same kind of compost recommended for outdoor ferneries, will be all that is necessary. A list of suitable Ferns is given further on. When the Ferns are planted they should be well watered. They will require this frequently; as the body of soil not being large will soon become dry, especially in hot weather. Very pretty window gardens may easily be prepared in this manner, and maintain an attractive appearance.

WINDOW CASES.

These are made on the principle of the window boxes, with glass all round and above, thus enclosing and protecting the plants from winds, storms, dust, and other adverse influences to which those in simple window boxes are exposed. The cases being built against the window access is obtained by lifting the sash. This may be raised the greater part of the day, but closed when necessary to prevent dust settling upon the plants; also when the room becomes hot from the burning of gas or from other cause.

During severe weather, if the sash be raised, the warmth of the room will help to keep the plants free from frost. The Ferns may either be planted in soil or kept in pots. When in the latter they will need water more frequently than when planted out, as the soil in a pot dries more quickly than a larger body filling the bottom of the case. If exposed to the sun the case must be shaded at al times when there is risk of the Ferns being scorched.

Section 9.

PROPAGATION.

FERNS may be propagated from buds produced on the fronds, from tubers and buds on the roots, from bulbils formed on their creeping sarmentum, by division of their crowns and rhizomes, and from spores. Adiantum caudatum, A. ciliatum, A. dolabriforme, A. lunulatum, many of the Aspleniums, Fadyenia prolifera, Goniopteris reptans, Polystichum lentum, P. proliferum, P. lepidocaulon, P. viviparum, and a few others, produce terminal buds. If the fronds are bent and pegged down so that the buds touch the soil, they will emit roots, and soon be sufficiently rooted to support themselves. At this stage they may be severed from the plant, and the frond allowed to resume its original position. The young plants will now require the same treatment as their parents, and will soon make nice specimens.

Phegopteris effusus, Woodwardia radicans and its varieties, produce several young plants on each frond. These may either be pegged down or taken off. If put into small pots in a frame, or covered by a glass to keep them close, they will soon have an abundance of roots, and send up young fronds.

Many Aspleniums, Lastrea prolifica, and Woodwardia orientalis, produce on the upper surface of their fronds a large number of tiny bulbils. These may be taken off when large enough to handle. They should then be pricked into pans of nice light compost, with a thin layer of silver sand on the top. After being carefully watered, so as not to wash them out of their places, they should be put in a frame or under a propagating glass, where they will soon make nice little plants.

Doryopteris palmata, Goniopteris vivipara, Hemionitis palmata, H. cordata, Stenosemia aurita, and a few others which produce buds on different parts of their fronds, should be pegged down to the surface of the soil, and the young plants will soon be ready to take off and to commence an independent existence.

Adiantum amabile (A. Mooreii) and A. diaphanum (A. setulosum) produce numberless little plants on their roots, both of them from buds formed there, the latter from tiny tubers as well.

Adiantum æthiopicum, A. assimile, A. formosum, A. palmatum, Asplenium planicaule, Hypolepis Bergiana, Struthiopteris Germanica, S. Pennsylvanica, and others, with underground rhizomes, may be propagated by carefully pulling them to pieces before they have commenced their new growth. Every piece of rhizome should have a growing point and as many roots as possible.

Nephrolepis Bauseii, N. Philippinensis, N. pluma, and N. tuberosa, produce tubers like small potatoes on their roots. When the plants are potted, the tubers should be collected and placed in a pot by themselves. In a short time they will begin to grow and develop into nice little plants.

Most of the Platyceriums form small buds on their roots These, if left until they have produced several barren fronds or shields, may then be taken off and planted by themselves.

The Nephrolepis send out a number of creeping stems (sarmentum), which produce bulbils at intervals. When on a damp surface these will emit roots, and soon become plants, which may be severed from the parent without injury. Several of the Blechnums and Aspleniums produce young plants in the same manner, though not to so great an extent. In all such cases the plants may be propagated readily by severing the creeping stems as soon as the young plants are sufficiently rooted.

Those species with rhizomes creeping above ground are easily propagated. This section comprises the Davallias, commonly called Hare's Foot and Squirrel's Foot Ferns, the Anapeltis, Drynarias, and many others. If the rhizomes be kept pegged close to the soil they root as they grow, and may be separated from the parent plant by first cutting through the rhizome and then carefully taking it up with all its roots attached, and two or three fronds. When planted they should be pegged and made secure, and they will soon become established. If the rhizomes have extended over the sides of the pot they will be destitute of roots. It will be useless to cut and plant these unless the rhizome is traced back a sufficient distance to take up with a number of roots attached. If this is not done the part which has grown over the side should be bent back, pegged on the soil, and left until it has produced roots, when it may be separated with little risk; or a pot containing soil might be placed under it, the rhizome pegged on, and left thus until rooted. There are many different species amenable to this mode of propagation, but in every case there must be a growing point to the rhizome, besides fibrous roots, and, when possible, several fronds.

Filmy Ferns, Hymenophyllæ and Trichomanes, may be propagated in this manner, but they must afterwards be kept very close and damp, where there is no evaporation to affect them. They should be in a glass frame, or under propagating glasses, until well rooted. All Ferns after being divided, are better placed in a close frame for awhile. Although many do not actually require it, they do not fee the disturbance so much, and they recover from the check much more quickly when so treated.

Gleichenias are the must difficult subjects to deal with by division. Large plants can rarely be divided successfully. It is only by securing the younger part of the rhizomes with fibrous roots and growing points that success is possible. The old portion of the rhizomes is valueless, only so far as its roots may help to support the whole. They seldom, if ever, break out again; hence, young, vigorous plants may be much more successfully manipulated.

Species such as Adiantum cuneatum and A. Farleyense, which form clusters of crowns, may be propagated by carefully pulling the crowns apart, retaining to each one every root possible. To facilitate the operation the soil should be gently shaken or washed away; the crowns must then be separated, the roots disentangled, and the plants potted at once to prevent their becoming dry. They should be kept close and shaded for a few days to prevent undue evaporation and loss of vigour. The plan of cutting through the crowns and ball of roots is a very bad one. It severs many roots from the crowns to which they belong, and this materially reduces the ability of the plants to survive. It is far better to take a little more trouble and separate the crowns, carefully retaining the roots as intact as possible. The best time for propagation by division in the various ways already described is February and March. The plants are then either entirely at rest or only just beginning to grow, and therefore do not suffer as they would when in full growth. Those with rhizomes may be divided when growing as well as when dormant, and they will not feel any ill effects if the instructions here given are followed.

Ferns, which grow by means of an upright caudex, as the Tree Ferns, and others which do not rise above the soil but keep to one crown, are not amenable to increase by division, but must be propagated from spores. Nearly every species produces spores, though some of them very sparingly, and a few varieties are quite sterile. There is a marked difference in the freedom of germination of some species and varieties as compared with others. There appears to be a law operating among them which in some mysterious manner restricts the production from spores of those kinds readily propagated by bulbils or by division of their rhizomes; while, on the other hand, those which can only be increased sparingly by division, may be raised in thousands from spores.

SPORES.

Propagation by spores is the most interesting of all means of increasing the stock of plants, and it is very wonderful from first to last.

COLLECTING SPORES.

The spores are contained in small sacs, arranged in clusters or lines at the back of the fronds; sometimes in large patches on certain parts of the fronds; at other times spread all over the surface; and in some species they are arranged along the edges. Some of the clusters are covered by a thin membrane, which lifts up as the spores approach maturity, rolls back, and sometimes falls off or shrivels up. In many species the clusters are not covered at all. When first formed the spore cases are colourless, then pale green, and as growth advances some become black, others green, and many of various shades of brown. When the covering (indusium) begins to lift, it is a sign that the spores are nearly ripe. The spore cases themselves swell, and when the spores in them are matured the cases burst and scatter their contents in the form of minute dust. Spores are of many colours—black, dark brown, light brown, golden yellow, and green. When ripe, the fronds, or that portion bearing the spores, should be cut off, wrapped in paper (white is the best), and put in a warm dry place. On the following day the fronds will be shrivelled; but lying on the paper there will be a dust-like substance, which proves to be innumerable spores. With these there will always be a multitude of spore-cases which have detached themselves from the frond in the act of bursting. A casual observer might take the whole to be spores, but an examination of the mass through a lens will soon reveal the difference. This is important, as those who are not acquainted with the difference often take care of the useless cases and neglect the finer substance, which is the only valuable part.

Spores should be sown as soon after collection as possible. If they are to be kept a long time they should be put into bottles and tightly corked, when some of them will retain their vitality for years.

SOWING THE SPORES.

Pots 4in. or 5in. in diameter are a convenient size in which to sow spores. They should have an inch of drainage at the bottom, two or three inches of bog broken small, a layer of compost like that used for the generality of Ferns, and on this a layer of soil which has been scalded or burned to destroy all germs of vegetable life which might be in it. As some spores germinate better on one substance than another it is well to vary the surface layer. In one pot it may be compost as mentioned above; in another, bits of brick or sandstone broken small; in another, small pieces of peat; and in another, loam in little lumps the size of a pea. Those who are not successful with one medium should try others for special kinds. The last layer should be about an inch from the top of the pot, and when this is in place the whole should be well watered. The spores must then be scattered very thinly over the surface. The sowing should be done in a perfectly still atmosphere, as the slightest draught will send the spores flying about the place.

The pots should have pieces of glass put over them as soon as each one is sown. These should be kept on continually to prevent the spores of other kinds getting in, and also to keep a close moist atmosphere about the spores. This helps them to germinate and grow more freely afterwards. A dry atmosphere retards growth and sometimes prevents it altogether.

The pots should be placed in saucers containing water. This will rise up the compost and keep it damp. Should it be necessary at any time to give water in any other way, it should be done by holding the pot in a pail of water, so that it may soak up and saturate the whole. The spores must not be watered overhead, as they would be disturbed and washed out of their places.

The pots containing spores of Exotic Ferns should be placed in a light position and in a temperature of 70°. Many will germinate in a considerably lower temperature, but they will be longer in developing.

Hardy Ferns may be sown in ordinary greenhouse temperature or in a frame, but in the latter they are slower in developing than when in a higher temperature.

Spores vary greatly in the time they take to commence growth. Some germinate in a day or two, others are months before there is any sign of progress. Even those taken from one frond will vary, some of them developing weeks before others sown at the same time and in the same pot.

The first indication of growth is a faint colouring of green on the soil. This increases until the surface is covered by a flat vegetable growth resembling liverwort in appearance. At this stage the mass should be separated into little patches, and planted in other pots filled with ordinary Fern compost. They may now be watered overhead with a very fine rose, covered again with glasses, and placed where they will receive plenty of light. They will require to be kept damp. In a short time tiny fronds will make their appearance. They will soon need further division, and eventually, when large enough to handle, they may be potted singly, to go on their Fern-life, developing beauty day by day, and soon bearing upon their own fronds the germs of another generation.

The process of development is full of interest and wonder. Not the least mysterious thing connected with the raising of Ferns from spores is that it is no unusual occurrence for a totally different kind to make its appearance in a pot from that sown in it. The stranger is sometimes in almost exclusive possession, while that which was expected is conspicuous by its absence. Even with the greatest care in sowing, many different kinds will afterwards be found in one pot, so that it is impossible to be sure of the species of the crop until the fronds are developed. Many wonderful and unaccountable facts might be referred to in connection with this subject, but it may be left with a warning to the sower not to be discouraged when matters do not turn out as expected, but to try again, when possibly an unexpected treasure may some day come up in the form of an entirely new variety.

Section 10.

SELECTIONS OF FERNS.
FIFTY CHOICE STOVE FERNS FOR POTS.

ADIANTUM æmulum, A. Bauseii, A. cardiochlœna, a large handsome species; A. concinnum, A. cultratum, A. dolabriforme, A. Farleyense, an exceedingly beautiful variety; A. Lathomii, specially handsome; A. macrophyllum, young fronds

ADIANTUM FARLEYENSE.

deep pink; A. Neo Caledoniæ, A reginæ, A. Sanctæ Catherinæ, A. speciosum, A. trapeziforme, a splendid

DAVALLIA PARVULA.

species of large growth; A. villosum, Aglaomorpha Meyeniana (the Bear's Paw Fern), Anemia adiantifolia,

GYMNOGRAMMA SCHIZOPHYLLA GLORIOSA.

Aspidium Plumierii, Asplenium Australasicum (the Bird's Nest Fern), A. Belangerii, A. formosum,

A. inæquale, A. laxum pumilum, A. nobilis, a light, feathery, and graceful variety; Blechnum gracile, Cheilanthes elegans (the Lace Fern), very beautiful; Davallia dissecta, D. Fijiensis, D. Griffithiana, D. parvula, very small fronds, finely cut, exceedingly pretty; D. retusa, Drynaria musæfolia, the veining very distinct; Gleichenia dichotoma, Gymnogramma Alstonii (Gold Fern), G. chrysophylla (Gold Fern), G. decomposita, fronds very finely cut; G. Peruviana argyrophylla (Silver Fern), G. schizophylla gloriosa, very beautiful,

NIPHOBOLUS HETERACTIS.

fronds cut into fine segments, of graceful drooping habit; Lygodium dichotomum, a magnificent climbing Fern; Nephrolepis davallioides, N. d. furcans, N. Duffii, N. exaltata, Niphobolus Heteractis, Onychium auratum, a very handsome species, fronds erect, finely cut; Pheg-opteris effusus, Phlebodium aureum, fronds large and deeply glaucous; Pteris tricolor, P. Victoriæ, very prettily variegated; Rhipidopteris peltata, small fronds, fan-shaped, deeply cut.

A Second Fifty Choice Stove Ferns for Pots.

Adiantum Aneitense, A. Collisii, A. concinnum latum, A. curvatum, A. flabellatum, A. Flemingii, A. Peruvianum, A. pulverulentum, A. rhodophyllum, A. Seemannii, A. tenerum, A. tetraphyllum gracile, A. Versaillense, dwarf fronds, branched and crested, very pretty; A.

PTERIS TRICOLOR.

Victoriæ, A. Weigandii, Anemia collina, Aspidium trifoliatum, Asplenium Baptistii, A. bifidum, A. horridum, A. obtusilobum, A. prolongatum, A. pteropus, A. viviparum, Blechnum latifolium, Campyloneurum brevifolium, Cheilanthes radiata, Davallia alpina, D. elegans, Doryopteris palmata, Elaphoglossum L'Herminierii (the

Silver Eel Fern), Gymnogramma calomelanos (Silver Fern), G. Laucheana (Gold Fern), G. Muellerii, G. Parsonsii, a dwarf, crested gold fern; G. Pearceii D. Fijiensis plumosa, a handsome variety, of large growth; D. fœniculacea, D. polyantha, D. pycnocarpa, robusta, very beautiful, finely-cut fronds; G. Wettenhalliana (Crested Sulphur Fern), Hymenodium crinitum (Elephant Ear Fern), Leucostegia affinis, Lygodictyon Forsterii (Climbing Fern), L. volubile (Climbing Fern),

NIPHOPSIS ANGUSTATUS.

Nephrolepis Bauseii, Niphopsis angustatus, Phlebodium sporodocarpum, Pleopeltis fossa, P. Xiphias.

TWENTY-FIVE BASKET FERNS FOR STOVE.

Adiantum amabile, sends its roots through the basket all round, young plants are produced on them, and their foliage soon forms a beautiful mass of green. A. caudatum, A. dolabriforme, A. Farleyense, A. fragrantissimum, A. Peruvianum, Asplenium longissimum, produces long pendent fronds, bearing a young plant at the tip of each; Davallia dissecta, D. dissecta elegans, D. elegans, D. Fijiensis, D. Fijiensis plumosa, D. Griffithiana, D. pentaphylla. Goniophlebium chnoodes, G. subauriculatum, one of the best Basket Ferns in cultivation, produces pendent fronds 6ft. to 10ft. long; G. verrucosum, Gymnogramma chrysophylla, a Gold Fern, which shows its beautiful yellow powder to advantage when suspended; G. Dobroydense (Gold Fern), G. schizophylla gloriosa, a very beautiful variety with drooping fronds, exquisitely cut; Nephrolepis davallioides, N. d. furcans, a splendid variety, with crested fronds; N. exaltata, N. pectinata, Phegopteris effusus.

TWENTY-FIVE CHOICE VARIETIES FOR PLANTING ON BLOCKS OF CORK FOR SUSPENDING.

Adiantum ciliatum, produces young plants at the tips of its fronds; these develop, and produce others at their tips, forming a graceful and pretty object; A. dolabriforme is like the preceding in habit, but its foliage is of deeper green. Asplenium nobilis, Davallia decora, D. dissecta, D. dissecta elegans, D. elegans, D. Fijiensis, D. F. major, D. F. plumosa, D. Griffithiana, D. heterophylla, D. pentaphylla, D. pycnocarpa, D. Tyermannii, Lopholepis piloselloides, Nephrolepis cordata compacta, N. pectinata, N. Philippinensis Oleandra nodosa, Phymatodes vulgaris cristata, Phlebodium venosum, Platycerium grande, P. Stemmaria, P. Willinckii. The Platyceriums should be suspended by one wire, the others by one or four wires, according to whether they are to hang against the wall or from the roof.

FIFTY STOVE FERNS FOR ROCKWORK.

Acrostichum osmundaceum, Adiantum Bauseii, A. cardiochloena, A. cultratum, A. Funckii, A. Lathomii, A. trapeziforme, Aglaomorpha Meyeniana, Aspidium dilaceratum, A. Plumierii, Asplenium Australasicum, A. Belangerii, A. horridum, A. inaequale, A. laxum pumilum, Campyloneurum phyllitidis, Davallia decora, D. dissecta, D. dissecta elegans, D. elegans, D. elegans polydactyla, D. Fijiensis, D. F. major, D. F. plumosa, D. ornata, D.

polyantha, D. retusa, Drynaria coronans, D. musæfolia, Goniophlebium neriifolium, Hypoderis Brownii, Lonchitis pubescens, Marattia elegans, Meniscium oligophyllum, Microsorum irioides, Nephrolepis davallioides, N. d. furcans, N. ensifolia, N. exaltata, N. Zollingeriana, Oleandra articulata, Olfersia cervina, Phegopteris effusus, Phlebodium aureum, P. sporodocarpum, Phymatodes nigrescens, Pleocnemia Leuzeana, Pleopeltis Xiphias, Polypodium leiorhizon, Stenochlæna scandens.

TWENTY-FIVE STOVE FERNS FOR WALLS.

Adiantum æmulum, A. amabile, A. capillus veneris, A. caudatum, A. cuneatum, A. dolabriforme, A. fragrantissimum, A. Peruvianum, A. tenerum, Asplenium alatum, A. planicaule, Davallia decora, D. dissecta, D. d. elegans, D. elegans, D. Fijiensis, D. F. major, D. pentaphylla, Goniophlebium appendiculatum, G. glaucophyllum, Leucostegia hirsuta, Nephrolepis cordata compacta, N. pectinata, Polypodium Catherinæ, Stenochlæna scandens.

TWELVE STOVE FERNS FOR CUTTING.

Adiantum æmulum, A. amabile, A. Farleyense, A. fragrantissimum, A. Lathomii, A. Neo Guinense, A. scutum, Davallia dissecta, D. d. elegans, D. Fijiensis, D. Griffithiana, D. Tyermannii.

TWELVE STOVE SELAGINELLAS.

Selaginella amœna, very pretty, light, and graceful; S. atrovirides, distinct, bronzy brown in colour; S. cæsia, beautiful trailing species of deep metallic blue; S. Emiliana, a "Bird's Nest" moss, very pretty; S. filicina, has large plumose fronds; S. gracilis, very pretty and graceful; S. grandis, exceedingly handsome, has large fan-shaped, spreading, bright green foliage; S. hæmatodes, light green, glossy, crimpy fronds; S. inæqualifolia, S. Lyallii, has light green crisp foliage; S. tassellata, very pretty and distinct; S. Willdenovii, commonly known as S. cæsia arborea and S. lævigata, a most beautiful species, of climbing habit, producing large pinnæ of a lovely metallic blue shade, the colour being most intense when the plant is growing in the shade, when its iridescence is very striking.

FIFTY WARM GREENHOUSE FERNS FOR POTS.

ADIANTUM capillus veneris, A. c.v. grande, A. c.v. O'Brienianum, A. ciliatum, A. colpodes elegans, A. cuneatum, A. c. grandiceps, A. decorum, A. gracillimum, A. Luddimannianum, A. Pacottii, A. palmatum, A. tinctum, young foliage

ADIANTUM DECORUM.

beautifully tinted; A. Williamsii, a very handsome variety, with pea-green foliage, the stems slightly powdered; Asplenium bulbiferum, A. Colensoii, A. fœniculaceum, Cheilanthes elegans, C. hirta, Davallia bullata (the Squirrel's Foot Fern), D. Canariensis (the Hare's Foot Fern), D. hemiptera, D. Mooreana, a handsome large-growing species; D. tenuifolia Veitchiana, a most beautiful variety, with gracefully drooping finely-cut fronds; Doodia aspera multifida, Gymnogramma ochracea (a Gold Fern), Lastrea Richardsii multifida Leucostegia immersa, Lomaria fluviatilis, L. L'Her-

CHEILANTHES ELEGANS.

minierii (a miniature Tree-Fern), young fronds a deep rose colour; Lygodium Japonicum, a climbing Fern of very free growth; L. palmatum, a climbing Fern of small growth but very pretty; Microlepia hirta cristata, a most handsome variety, produces large fronds, light green in colour, heavily crested; Onychium Japonicum, Osmunda Japonica corymbifera, a pretty, dwarf, crested,

Royal Fern; Platycerium alcicorne, a Stag's Horn Fern; Polypodium hastatum, Polystichum viviparum, Pteris argyrea, prettily variegated; P. cretica, P. c. nobilis, a handsome, densely-crested variety; P. Mayii, very pretty, dwarf, variegated crested; P. semipinnata, P. serrulata densa, heavily crested, graceful and pretty; P. s. fastigiata, P. tremula. P. t. Smithiana, fronds branched and heavily-crested, very distinct; P. umbrosa,

ASPLENIUM ZEYLANICUM.

P. Victoriæ, a pretty, light, variegated variety; Sadleria cyatheoides, a very handsome species, with large, gracefully-arching fronds, coriaceous in texture, dark green.

A SECOND FIFTY WARM GREENHOUSE FERNS
FOR POTS.

Adiantum cuneatum elegans, A. Lawsonianum, fronds finely cut; A. excisum multifidum, a heavily-crested variety; A. hispidulum (pubescens), A. Mariesii, a handsome variety, very distinct; A. pedatum, a beautiful variety of free growth; A. reniforme, A. Veitchii, A. venustum, Alsophila Rebeccæ, Asplenium bifolium, A. caudatum, A. flaccidum, has drooping fronds, very graceful; A. lucidum, a handsome variety, with bright green glossy foliage; A. præmorsum laceratum, Balantium culcita, Blechnum platyptera, a small Tree-Fern, of very fine appearance; Brainea insignis, Cheilanthes tomentosa, Cibotium Barometz, a large growing species, of handsome appearance; Davallia Canariensis pulchella, D. Mariesii, a beautiful variety, with finely-cut fronds; D. tenuifolia, D. Tyermannii, Dictyogramma Japonica variegata, Diplazium Shepherdii, D. Thwaitesii, Doodia caudata, D. media crispa cristata, Hypolepis Bergiana, Lastrea aristata variegata, L. fragrans, the (Violet-scented Fern), a pretty dwarf species; Leucostegia chærophylla, Lomaria ciliata, a miniature Tree-Fern; L. gibba, a handsome small Tree-Fern; Lygodium scandens, a very pretty Climbing Fern, evergreen, has light green foliage and is of free growth; Nephrodium molle corymbiferum, Niphobolus Lingua corymbifera, a distinct, dwarf, heavily-crested variety, foliage very leathery; Nothoclœna Newberryii, distinct and beautiful, foliage covered with silvery-white hairs; N. sinuata, very pretty, long, narrow drooping fronds, silvery underneath; Osmunda palustris, a pretty, evergreen Royal Fern; Pellæa ternifolia, fronds narrow, very glaucous; Polystichum vestitum venustum, Pteris cretica alba lineata, prettily variegated; P. c. magnifica, heavily crested; P. serrulata cristata, P. s.c. plumosa, has dense drooping foliage; P. s. major, a large variety of the Ribbon Fern; P. s. major cristata, a large variety, crested; P. tremula crispa.

Twelve Basket Ferns for Warm Greenhouse.

Adiantum assimile, a beautiful variety, its underground rhizomes spread through the basket and produce on all sides a mass of lovely pale-green foliage. A. cuneatum grandiceps, a crested variety of the common Maidenhair, distinct and handsome; A. gracillimum, foliage exceedingly fine, and, when young, has a lovely tint; A. palmatum, a very beautiful variety, with gracefully-drooping fronds; A. Williamsii, Asplenium flaccidum, fronds drooping and graceful; A. longissimum, produces pendent fronds six feet long, and makes a handsome specimen; Blechnum glandulosum, Davallia dissecta elegans, D. Mooreana, has large fronds of fine appearance; D. tenuifolia Veitchiana, a lovely variety, with graceful light foliage; Microlepia hirta cristata, has large, pale-green, heavily-crested fronds.

TWELVE WARM GREENHOUSE FERNS FOR BLOCKS OF CORK SUSPENDED.

Adiantum assimile cristatum, A. ciliatum, A. æmulum, A. fragrantissimum, A. setulosum, Davallia Tyermannii, Nephrolepis pectinata, Oleandra nodosa, Pellæa ternifolia, Platycerium Willinckii, Pteris serrulata Hendersonii, P. s. plumosa.

FIFTY WARM GREENHOUSE FERNS FOR ROCKWORK.

Adiantum decorum, A. formosum, A. Mariesii, A. pedatum, Asplenium fœniculaceum, A. præmorsum, A. p. laceratum, Blechnum Atherstonii, B. polypodiodes, Cibotium Barometz, Davallia Canariensis, D. Mooreana, D. tenuifolia, D. t. stricta, Dennstædtia davallioides, Diplazium dilatatum, Drynaria pustulata, Hypolepis repens, Lastrea dissecta, L. frondosa, L. patens superba, L. Richardsii multifida, Lepicystis sepulta, L. squamata, Leucostegia immersa, Litobrochia vespertilionis, Lomaria gibba, Microlepia hirta cristata, M. platyphilla, a large handsome species; M. strigosa, Nephrodium molle, Niphobolus lingua, Onychium Japonicum, Osmunda Japonica corymbifera, O. palustris, Phegopteris trichodes, Polypodium Billardierii, Polystichum Capense, Pteris argyrea, P. cretica, P. c. cristata, P. longifolia, P. longifolia nobilis, P. scaberula, P. serrulata, P. s. major, P. s. major cristata, P. tremula, P. umbrosa, Todea Africana.

TWENTY-FIVE WARM GREENHOUSE FERNS FOR WALLS.

Adiantum assimile, A. ciliatum, A. colpodes, A. cuneatum, A. c. grandiceps, A gracillimum, A. pentaphyllum, A. pubescens, A. setulosum, Asplenium Colensoii, A.

flaccidum, Blechnum glandulosum, Davallia hemiptera, D. Mooreana, D. Tyermannii, Osmunda palustris, Pellæa ternifolia, Platyceriumalcicorne, Polypodium Billardierii, Polystichum mucronatum, Pteris semipinnata, Selaginella caulescens argentea, S. Martensii, S. pubescens, S. stolonifera.

Twenty-five Warm Greenhouse Ferns for Cutting.

Adiantum capillus veneris, A. colpodes elegans, A. cuneatum, A. cuneatum elegans, A decorum, A. gracillimum, A. Mariesii, A. pedatum, A. Williamsii, Davallia bullata, D. decora, D. dissecta, D. d. elegans, D. Mariesii, D. Tyermannii, Leucostegia immersa, Nephrodium molle, Onychium Japonicum, Osmunda palustris, Pteris cretica, P. c. cristata, P. serrulata, P. s. cristata, P. tremula, Selaginella pubescens.

Twelve Selaginellas for Warm Greenhouse.

Selaginella caulescens argentea, S. delicatissima, S. densa, S. divaricata, S. involvens, S. Japonica, S. Kraussiana, S. K. aurea, S. K. variegata, S. Martensii, S. pubescens, S. variabilis.

Fifty Cool Greenhouse Ferns for Pots.

ADIANTUM Æthiopicum, A. affine, A. capillus veneris, A. colpodes elegans, A. decorum, A. formosum, A. Mariesii, A. pedatum, A. Williamsii, Alsophila excelsa, Asplenium bulbiferum, A. Hemionitis, A. lucidum, A. præmorsum lacera-

ADIANTUM PEDATUM.

tum, Athyrium laxum, Cheilanthes Clevelandii, C. gracillima, Cyrtomium caryotidium, C. falcatum, Davallia bullata, D. Mariesii, Dicksonia antarctica, D. squarrosa, Doodia aspera, D. a. multifida, Gleichenia dicarpa, G. flabellata, G. Speluncia, Gymnogramma triangularis, Lastrea erythrosora, L. fragrans, Leucostegia immersa, Lomaria attenuata, Lomaria falcata bipinnatifida, L. fluviatilis, Lygodium Japonica, Microlepia platyphylla, Nephrodium molle, N. molle corymbiferum, Nothoclœna lanuginosa, N. Newberryi, Onychium

GLEICHENIA SEMIVESTITA.

Japonicum, Osmunda Japonica corymbifera, Platyloma cordata, Polystichum concavum, P. vestitum venustum, Pteris cretica, P. scaberula, Woodwardia radicans, W. radicans crispa.

A SECOND FIFTY COOL GREENHOUSE FERNS FOR POTS.

Adiantum capillus veneris grande, A. Chilense, A. digitatum, A. reniforme, A. venustum, Aleuritopteris Mexicana, Anemidictyon phyllitides, Asplenium bifolium, A. Hemionitis cristatum, A. monanthemum, Blechnum

Atherstonii, Cheilanthes fragrans, Davallia Mariesii cristata, D. Novæ Zealandiæ, Dictyogramma Japonica, D. J. variegata, Gleichenia dicarpa longipinnata, G. semivestita, Hypolepis distans, Lastrea glabella, L. opaca, Lomaria Banksii, L. discolor, L. pumila, Lomariopsis heteromorpha, Lygodium palmatum, Microlepia strigosa, Mohria thurifraga, Nephrodium Sangwellii, Niphobolus lingua, Nothoclœna cretacea, N. Marantæ, N. sinuata, Osmunda palustris, Pellæa andromedæfolia, P. ornithopus Polypodium hastatum, P. incanum, P. Scoulerii, Polystichum Tsus-Simense, Pteris cretica, cristata, P. longifolia, P. serrulata cristata, P. . major, P. s. major cristata, P. tremula, Todea Africana, Woodsia mollis, Woodwardia radicans Burgessiana, W. r. cristata.

TWELVE BASKET FERNS FOR COOL GREENHOUSE.

Adiantum æthiopicum, A. assimile, A. decorum, Blechum polypodioides, Leucostegia immersa, Osmunda palustris, Platycerium alcicorne, Pteris cretica, P. c. cristata, P. scaberula, Woodwardia radicans, W. r. cristata.

TWELVE FERNS FOR CORK BLOCKS IN COOL GREENHOUSE.

Adiantum capillus veneris, A. colpodes elegans, Cheilanthes elegans, Davallia bullata, D. Mariesii, D. m. cristata, Hypolepis distans, Pellæa ternifolia, Polystichum triangulum laxum, Pteris cretica magnifica, P. serrulata, P. s. cristata.

TWENTY-FIVE COOL GREENHOUSE FERNS FOR WALLS.

Adiantum æthiopicum, A. capillus veneris, A. c. v. grande, A. colpodes elegans, A. decorum, A. Mariesii, A. venustum, A. Williamsii, Blechnum polypodioides, Cyrtomium caryotidium, C. falcatum, Davallia bullata, D. Mariesii, Diplazium Thwaitesii, Drynaria pustulata, Niphobolus Lingua, Onychium Japonicum, Polystichum acrostichoides, P. triangulum laxum, Pteris cretica, P. c. cristata, P. scaberula, P. serrulata, P. s. cristata, Selaginella Martensii.

Twelve Cool Greenhouse Ferns for Cutting.

Adiantum capillus veneris, A. decorum, A. Mariesii, A. Pacottii, A. pedatum, Davallia bullata, D. Mariesii, Onychium Japonicum, Pteris cretica, P. c. cristata, P. serrulata, P. s. cristata.

Twelve Cool Greenhouse Selaginellas.

Selaginella Brownii, S. denticulata, S. Douglassii, S. involvens, S. Japonica, S. Kraussiana, S. K. aurea, S. K. variegata, S. Martensii, S. Oregana, S. Poulterii, S. pubescens.

Fifty Cold Greenhouse Ferns for Pots.

ADIANTUM affine, A. capillus veneris, A. c. v. daphnites, A. emarginatum, A. pedatum, Aspidium cristatum Floridanum, Asplenium angustifolium, A. fissum, A. fontanum, Athyrium goringianum pictum, Botrychium Virginicum, Camptosorus rhizophyllus, Cyrtomium falcatum, C. Fortuneii, Cystopteris bulbifera, Davallia Mariesii, Dennstædtia punctilobula, Dicksonia antarctica, Dictyo-

ADIANTUM PEDATUM.

gramma Japonica, Gymnogramma triangularis, Lastrea atrata, L. decurrens, L. fragrans, L. opaca, L. prolifica, L. Sieboldii, Lomaria Chilensis, L. crenulata, L. pumila, Lygodium Japonicum, L. palmatum, Niphobolus lingua, Onoclea sensibilis, Onychium Japonicum, Osmunda Japonica corymbifera, O. palustris, Pellæa atropurpurea, Polystichum acrostichoides, P. concavum, P. proliferum, P. setosum, P. triangulum laxum, P. vestitum venustum,

Pteris scaberula, Struthiopteris Germanica, Todea Africana, Woodsia ilvensis, W. obtusa, Woodwardia radicans, W. r. cristata.

ASPLENIUM FONTANUM.

A SECOND FIFTY COLD GREENHOUSE FERNS FOR POTS.

Adiantum c. v. grande, Aspidium juglandifolium, A. pilosum, Asplenium adulterinum, A. ebeneum, A. Seelosii,

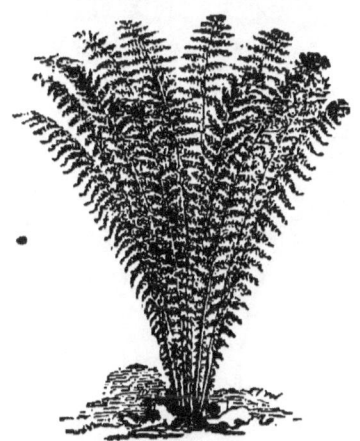

STRUTHIOPTERIS GERMANICA.

Cyrtomium caryotidium, Davallia bullata, D. Mariesii cristata, D. Novæ Zealandiæ, Dicksonia squarrosa, Dictyogramma Japonica variegata, Lastrea frondosa, Lomaria alpina, Platyloma falcata, P. rotundifolia, Struthiopteris Pennsylvanica recurva, Woodsia polystichoides Veitchii, Woodwardia Japonica, W. radicans crispa, Allosorus

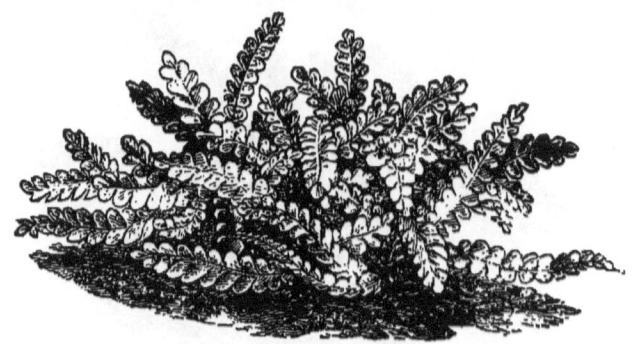

LOMARIA ALPINA.

acrostichoides, Aspidium Nevadense, A. rigidum argutum, Lastrea Goldiana, Osmunda cinnamomea, O. Claytoniana, O. gracilis, Polystichum munitum.

POLYPODIUM VULGARE TRICHOMANOIDES.

The following are British: Asplenium lanceolatum, A. marinum, A. septentrionale, A. trichomanes confluens,

A. t. incisum, Athyrium F.f. corymbiferum, A. F.f. Edwardsii, A. F.f. Frizellæ, A. F.f. Kalothrix, A. F.f. plumosum elegans, A. F.f. Victoriæ, Blechnum spicant cristatum, Lastrea pseudo-mas cristata fimbriata, Polypodium v. Cambricum, P. v. trichomanoides, Polystichum angulare Bayliæ, Scolopendrium vulgare crispum, S. v.c. fimbriatum, S. v. cristulatum, S. v. laceratum, S. v. grandiceps, S. v. ramo-marginatum.

TWELVE BASKET FERNS FOR COLD GREENHOUSE.

Adiantum pedatum, Athyrium F.f. corymbiferum, A. F.f. Victoriæ, Osmunda palustris, Polystichum angulare, P. a. divisilobum acutum, P. a. d. decorum, P. a. proliferum, P. a. venustum, Woodwardia radicans, W. r. Burgessiana, W. r. cristata.

SCOLOPENDRIUM VULGARE CRISPUM.

TWENTY-FIVE COLD GREENHOUSE FERNS FOR WALLS.

Adiantum capillus veneris, A. pedatum, Asplenium nigrum, A. marinum, Lastrea æmula, L. prolifica, L. Sieboldii, Polypodium falcatum, P. vulgare, P. v. Cambricum, P. v. elegantissimum, P. v. trichomanoides, Polystichum acrostichoides, P. aculeatum, P. angulare, P. a. Bayliæ, P. a. divisilobum, P. a. proliferum, P. munitum, P. setosum, Scolopendrium vulgare, S. v. crispum, Selaginella Oregana, Woodwardia radicans, W. r. cristata.

Ferns and Fern Culture.

HALF-A-DOZEN COLD GREENHOUSE FERNS FOR CUTTING.

Adiantum capillus veneris, A. pedatum, Asplenium adiantum nigrum, Onychium Japonicum, Polystichum angulare, P. a. Bayliæ.

HALF-A-DOZEN SELAGINELLAS FOR COLD GREENHOUSE.

Selaginella denticulata, S. Japonica, S. Kraussiana, S. K. aurea, S. K. variegata, S. Oregana.

TODEA PELLUCIDA.

TWENTY-FIVE FILMY FERNS FOR COOL GREENHOUSE.

In order to have Filmy Ferns in the greatest perfection, they should be in a very close, damp atmosphere; therefore, unless the house is such as to provide this, they should be enclosed in a frame, or placed under glass shades. Hymenophyllum æruginosum, a beautiful variety, having a soft, downy appearance; H. caudiculatum, has long tapering fronds, very pretty; H.

Chiloense, dwarf in habit, small fronds; H. crispatum, fronds six inches long, erect, light green, crispy in appearance; H. demissum, light, graceful fronds, nine inches in length; H. d. nitens, smaller than the preceding, compact, and very pretty; H. flexuosum, a beautiful variety, fronds six to nine inches long, crimpy; Todea Fraserii, very handsome, large, light green arching fronds; T. grandipinnula, a splendid variety, with massive foliage, very pellucid; T. pellucida, a free-

TODEA SUPERBA.

growing species, produces fronds two feet long; T. superba, a most beautiful species, the fronds thick, mossy, cut into fine segments; T. Wilkesiana, a handsome species, which forms a thin stem and becomes a Tree-Fern; Trichomanes Alabamensis, a dwarf and pretty species; T. angustatum, fronds four inches long, cut into fine hair-like segments; T. auriculatum, a beautiful species, with drooping fronds six inches long, deeply lobed; T. Luschnathianum, resembles the preceding, but is more cut; T. maximum, produces large handsome fronds; T. radicans (the "Killarney Fern"), has triangular fronds, several times divided, very beautiful; T. r. Andrewsii, T. r. crispum, T. r. dilatatum, T. r. dissectum, four varieties of the "Killarney Fern," with various distinct characteristics; T. reniforme (the New Zealand Kidney Fern), a beautiful species, with kidney-shaped fronds; T. trichoidium, a lovely species, fronds four inches long, cut into hair-like segments; T. venosum, a dwarf and pretty species.

HALF-A-DOZEN FILMY FERNS FOR COLD GREENHOUSE.

Hymenophyllum demissum, H. d. nitens, H. Tunbridgense, H. Wilsonii, Todea pellucida, and Todea superba. Although these will bear a few degrees of frost, it is advisable to protect them, so as to keep the frost from them.

TWELVE STOVE FERNS FOR EXHIBITION.

ADIANTUM cardiochlæna, A. Farleyense, A. trapeziforme, Asplenium Australasicum, A. longissimum, Davallia Fijiensis plumosa, Goniophlebium subauriculatum, Gymnogramma chrysophylla, G. Peruviana argyrophylla, Nephrolepis davallioides furcans, N. rufescens tripinnatifida, Platycerium grande.

A SECOND TWELVE STOVE FERNS FOR EXHIBITION.

Adiantum Flemingii, A. fragrantissimum, A. Lathomii, Aglaomorpha Meyeniana, Asplenium laxum pumilum, Davallia Fijiensis, Gymnogramma schizophylla gloriosa, Nephrolepis davallioides, Phlebodium aureum, Phegopteris effusus, Platycerium Stemmaria, Stenochlœna scandens.

TWELVE GREENHOUSE FERNS FOR EXHIBITION.

Adiantum cuneatum, A. gracillimum, A. Williamsii, Davallia Mooreana, D. tenuifolia Veitchiana, D. Tyermannii, Gleichenia flabellata, G. rupestris, G. Speluncæ, Lomaria gibba, Microlepia hirta cristata, Woodwardia radicans.

A SECOND TWELVE GREENHOUSE FERNS FOR EXHIBITION.

Adiantum cuneatum grandiceps, A. decorum, A. pedatum, A. Veitchii, Blechnum platyptera, Brainea insignis, Davallia bullata, Gleichenia dicarpa longipinnata, G. Mendellii, G. semivestita, Pteris scaberula, Woodwardia radicans cristata.

Ferns and Fern Culture.

TWELVE HARDY EXOTIC FERNS FOR EXHIBITION.

Adiantum pedatum, Cyrtomium falcatum Fensomii, Lomaria Chilensis, Onoclea sensibilis, Osmunda cinnamomea, O. Claytoniana, O. gracilis, Polystichum Braunii, P. proliferum, P. munitum, Struthiopteris Germanica, S. orientalis.

TWELVE DWARF BRITISH FERNS FOR EXHIBITION.

Adiantum capillus veneris grande, Asplenium Germanicum, A. lanceolatum microdon, A. septentrionale, A. trichomanes confluens, A. t. cristatum, A. t. incisum,

ASPLENIUM TRICHOMANES CRISTATUM.

Athyrium Filix fœmina Edwardsii, Blechnum spicant cristatum, B. s. plumosum (serratum, Airey's No. 1), B. s. trinervo coronans, Polypodium vulgare trichomanoides.

A SECOND TWELVE DWARF BRITISH FERNS FOR EXHIBITION.

Asplenium marinum plumosum, Athyrium F. f. crispum, A. F.f. Vernoniæ. cristatum, Blechnum s. Maunderii, Lastrea montana congesta, Polypodium v. Cornubiense Fowlerii, P. v. elegantissimum, P. v. crista-

tum, Polystichum lonchitis, Scolopendrium vulgare
Coolingii, S. v. cristulatum, S. v. ramo-marginatum.

A THIRD TWELVE DWARF BRITISH FERNS FOR
EXHIBITION.

Adiantum capillus veneris, Asplenium marinum,
Blechnum s. lineare, Ceterach o. crenatum, Cystopteris
regia (alpina), C. montana, Polypodium v. pulcherrimum,
P. v. grandiceps, Lastrea montana ramo-coronans, L.
pseudo-mas ramulosissima, Scolopendrium vulgare conglomeratum, S. v. cristatum.

TWELVE BRITISH FERNS FOR EXHIBITION (NOT DWARF).

Athyrium F.f. acrocladon, A. F.f. Kalothrix, A. F.f.
plumosum, A. F.f. p. elegans, A. F.f. Victoriæ, Lastrea
F.m. fluctuosa, L. F.m. grandiceps, Lastrea pseudo-mas
cristata fimbriata, L. p.m. ramosissima, Osmunda regalis
cristata, Polystichum angulare plumosum, Scolopendrium
v. crispum fimbriatum.

A SECOND TWELVE BRITISH FERNS FOR EXHIBITION
(NOT DWARF).

Athyrium F.f. corymbiferum, A. F.f. Craigii, A. F.f.
Fieldæ, A. F.f. setigerum, A. F.f. todeoides, Lastrea F.m.
Bollandiæ, L. pseudo-mas cristata, L. p.m. cristata
angustata, Polypodium v. Cambricum, Scolopendrium
v. crispum, S. v. grandiceps, S. v. ramo-cristatum majus.

A THIRD TWELVE BRITISH FERNS FOR EXHIBITION.

Athyrium F.f. Frizellæ, A. F.f. glomeratum, A. F.f.
Grantæ, A. F.f. Pritchardii, A. F.f. ramo-cristatum,
Osmunda regalis, Polystichum angulare cristato-gracile,
P. a. cristatum, P. a. divisilobum decorum, P. a.
grandiceps, P. a. proliferum, Scolopendrium v. crispum
Stableræ.

FERNS SUITABLE FOR CULTIVATION IN DWELLING-
HOUSES.

SPLENIUM bifolium, A. bulbiferum, A. Colensoii, A. fœniculaceum, Davallia Canariensis, Cyrtomium falcatum, Lastrea p.m. cristata, Nephrodium molle, Nephrolepis exaltata, Platycerium alcicorne, Polystichum setosum, Pteris cretica, P. c. magnifica, P. c. nobilis, P. serrulata, P. s. cristata, P. s. major, P. s. major cristata, P. Ouvrardii, P. tremula, Polystichum ang. Bayliæ, P. a. proliferum densum, P, munitum, Scolopendrium v. crispum, S. v. laceratum. S. v. grandiceps.

Where there is no gas the following may be cultivated: Adiantum cuneatum, A. decorum, A. gracillimum, A. Williamsii.

FERNS SUITABLE FOR FERN STANDS.

As the stands are usually small, it is a good plan to have one nice sized Fern in the centre, and either a carpet of Selaginella or a few Dwarf Ferns planted round it. The following are all small-growing kinds. Those with (c) affixed are suitable for planting in the centre.

Adiantum capillus veneris (c), A. c. v. grande (c), A. c. v. O'Brienianum (c), A. hispidulum tenellum, A. reniforme, A. setulosum, Asplenium inæquale (c), A. obtusilobum, A. Fernandezianum, A. fontanum, A. monanthemum (c), A. præmossum laceratum (c), A. resectum, A. rutæfolium (c), A. tenellum, Anapeltis nitida, Davallia alpina, Doodia caudata, Lomaria alpina, Pteris internata, P. serrulata cristata, Selaginella amœna, S. Brownii, S. divaricata, S. Emiliana, S. Japonica, S. Kraussiana, S. K. aurea (golden), S. K. variegata (silvery), S. Martensii.

British varieties: Asplenium marinum, A. nigrum, A. trichomanes, Polystichum angulare Bayliæ (c), Scolopendrium v. Coolingii, S. v. cristulatum (c), S. v. densum.

Filmy Ferns: Hymenophyllum demissum (c), H. d. nitens, H. Tunbridgense, H. Wilsonii, Trichomanes Alabamensis, T. angustatum, T. radicans (c), T. reniforme (c), T. venosum.

FERNS SUITABLE FOR WARDIAN OR FERN CASES.

All those named as suitable for Fern stands, also, Adiantum affine, A. Mariesii, Arthropteris obliterata, Asplenium attenuatum, A. alatum, A. fragrans, A. Hemionitis, A. Colensoii, A. Zeylanicum, Blechnum gracile, Davallia bullata, D. Canariensis, D. C. pulchella, D. hemiptera, D. Novæ Zealandiæ, D. pentaphylla, Doodia amœna, D. media crispa cristata, Drynaria pustulata, Niphobolus Lingua, Onychium Japonicum, Phlebodium venosum, Polypodium adnascens, P. Billardierii, P. Scoulerii, Polystichum setosum, Pteris cretica and its varieties, P. internata, P. serrulata and its varieties, Rhipidopteris peltata, Selaginella caulescens, S. gracilis, S. grandis, S. umbrosa, S. Victoriæ, S. pubescens.

British varieties: Lastrea F.m. cristata, Polypodium v. Cambricum, P. v. elegantissimum, Polystichum angulare cristatum, P. a. grandiceps, P. a. perserratum, Scolopendrium v. crispum, S. v. cristatum, S. laceratum, S. v. grandiceps, S. v. ramo-cristatum, S. v. ramo-marginatum.

Filmy Ferns: Those recommended for Fern stands also, Hymenophyllum æruginosum, H. caudiculatum, H. Chiloense, H. flexuosum, H. pectinatum, Todea grandipinnula, T. pellucida, T. superba, Trichomanes auriculatum, T. exsectum, T. humile, T. maximum, T. m. umbrosum, T. radicans and its varieties, T. rigidum, T. trichoidium.

FERNS SUITABLE FOR WINDOW CASES.

Adiantum capillus veneris, A. pedatum, Asplenium ebeneum, A. fontanum, A. nigrum, A. trichomanes, Athyrium, F.f. Edwardsii, A. F.f. Vernoniæ cristatum,

A. F.f. Victoriæ, A. goringianum pictum, Blechnum s. cristatum, B. s. trinervo coronans, Cyrtomium caryotidium, C. falcatum, C. Fortuneii, Cystopteris bulbifera, Dictyogramma Japonica variegata, Lastrea atrata, L. decurrens, L. fragrans, L. opaca, L. prolifica, L. Sieboldii, L. p. m. cristata, L. p. m. crispa cristata, Lomaria alpina, Lygodium Japonicum, Niphobolus Lingua, Onoclea sensibilis, Onychium Japonicum, Polypodium vulgare Cambricum, P. v. cornubiense Fowlerii, P. v. elegantissimum, P. v. grandiceps, Polystichum acrosticboides, P. Braunii, P. munitum, P. setosum, P. angulare Bayliæ, P. a. cristatum, P. a. gracile, P. a. grandiceps, Pteris cretica, P. longifolia, Scolopendrium v. capitatum, S. v. crispum, S. v. cristatum, S. v. laceratum, S. v. grandiceps, S. v. ramo-marginatum, Todea Africana.

The Ferns here named are hardy enough to bear a few degrees of frost without injury, but means should be taken to keep the frost from them, so as to preserve their foliage as perfect as possible.

FERNS FOR WINDOW BOXES.

Twelve dwarf: Allosorus crispus, Asplenium nigrum, A. trichomanes, A. viride, Blechnum spicant, Ceterach officinarum, Cystopteris fragilis, Polypodium calcareum, P. dryopteris, P. phegopteris, P. vulgare, Polystichum onchitis.

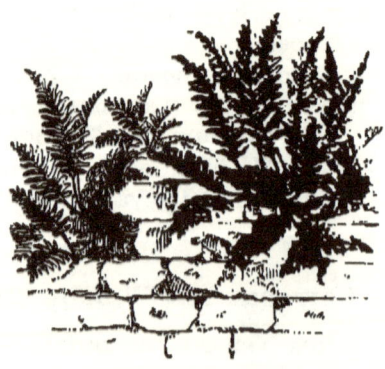

POLYPODIUM VULGARE.

Twelve medium size : Aspidium rigidum argutum, Lastrea æmula, L. intermedia, L. marginale, L. rigida, L. spinulosa, Polystichum acrostichoides, P. Braunii, Scolopendrium vulgare, S. v. crispum, S. v. grandiceps, Woodwardia angustifolia.

Twelve large size : Athyrium Filix fœmina, A. F.f. corymbiferum, A. F.f. Fieldiæ, Lastrea dilatata, L. Filixmas, L. F.m. fluctuosa, L. p.m. cristata, L. montana, Osmunda gracilis, Polystichum aculeatum, P. angulare, P. munitum.

TREE-FERNS FOR GREENHOUSE.

Large-growing species: Alsophila Australis, A. excelsa, A. Rebeccæ, Cibotium regale, C. Schiedii, C. spectabile, Cyathea dealbata (the New Zealand Silver Tree-Fern), C. medularis, C. princeps, Dicksonia antarctica, D. fibrosa, D. squarrosa.

Smaller-growing species: Blechnum Braziliense, B. Corcovadense, B. platyptera, Lomaria attenuata, L. ciliata, L. discolor, L. falcata, L.f. bipinnatifida, L. gibba, L. g. tincta, L. L'Herminierii (very dwarf), Sadleria cyatheoides.

HARDY FERNS FOR OUTDOOR FERNERIES.

Dwarf species and varieties growing from four inches to one foot in height

NORTH AMERICAN.—Allosorus acrostichoides, Aspidium Nevadense, Asplenium ebeneum, Cystopteri bulbifera, Lomaria alpina, Phegopteris hexagonoptera, Woodsia ilvensis, W. obtusa, Woodwardia angustifolia.

BRITISH.—Allosorus crispus (Parsley Fern), Asplenium adiantum nigrum (the Black Maidenhair Spleenwort), A. ruta-muraria (the Rue-leafed Spleenwort), A. trichomanes (the Black-stemmed Spleenwort), A. viride (the Green-stemmed Spleenwort), Athyrium F.f. crispum, A. F.f. Edwardsii, A. F.f. Findlayanum, A. F.f. Frizellæ, A. F.f. minimum, A. F.f. Vernoniæ, A. F.f. Vernoniæ cristatum, Blechnum spicant (the Hard Fern), B. s. imbricatum, Ceterach officinarum (the Scaly Spleenwort), C. o. crenatum, Cystopteris fragilis (the Brittle Bladder Fern), C. f. Dickieana, C. montana (the Mountain Bladder Fern), Lastrea pseudo-mas crispa, L. p.m. crispa cristata, Lastrea rigida (the Rigid Buckler Fern), Polypodium dryopteris (the Oak Fern), P. phegopteris (the Beech Fern), P. Robertianum (syn. calcareum, the Limestone Polypody), P. vulgare cornubiense Fowlerii, P. v. elegantissimum, Polystichum ang. Bayliæ, P. a. parvissimum, P. a. proliferum densum, P. lonchitis (the Holly Fern), Scolopendrium vulgare (the Hartstongue Fern), S. v. Coolingii, S. v. cristulatum, S. v. densum, S. v. digitatum, S. v. endivæfolium, S. v. fissum, S. v. grandiceps, S. v. marginatum tenuæ, S. v. ramo-cristatum.

SCOLOPENDRIUM VULGARE.

Medium-sized species and varieties which grow from one to two feet in height.

NORTH AMERICAN.—Aspidium cristatum, A. Noveboracense, A. rigidum argutum, Asplenium thelypterioides, Dennstædtia punctilobula, Lastrea intermedia, L. marginale, Onoclea sensibilis, Polystichum acrostichoides P. Braunii, Woodwardia Virginica, Struthiopteris Germanica (European).

BRITISH.—Athyrium F.f. capitatum, A. F.f. cristatum, A. F.f. Fieldæ, A. F.f. Frizellæ cristatum, A. F.f. irdlestoneii, A. F.f. Kilmoryensis, A. F.f. Mooreii, A. F.f. polydactylum, A. F.f. princeps, A. F.f. pulcherrimum, A. F.f. Smithii, A. F.f. stipatum, Lastrea æmula (the

Hay-scented Fern), L. dilatata cristato-gracile, L. d.
lepidota, L. Filix-mas fluctuosa, L. pseudo-mas Crouchii,
L. montana (the Mountain Buckler Fern, syn. L.
oreopteris), L. thelypteris (the Marsh Fern), Polypodium
alpestre, P. a. flexile, P. vulgare auritum, P. v. Cambricum
(the Welsh Polypody), P. v. crenatum, P. v. semilacerum
(the Irish Polypody), Polystichum aculeatum (the hard
Prickly Shield Fern), P. angulare acutilobum, P. a.
cristatum, P. a. divisilobum acutum, P. a. grandidens, P.
a. imbricatum, P. a. lineare, P. a. perserratum, P. a.
polydactylum, P. a. proliferum, P. a. p. Wollastonii, P.
a. rotundatum, P. a. Wakeleyanum, Scolopendrium v.
capitatum, S. v. crispum, S. v. multifidum.

*Large species and varieties growing two feet high
and upwards.*

NORTH AMERICAN.—Aspidium cristatum Clintonianum, A. spinulosum Bootii, Athyrium Michauxii, Lastrea Goldiana, Osmunda cinnamomea, produces its fertile fronds in the centre of the plant, entirely distinct from the barren; the spore cases, when matured, are cinnamon-coloured and very attractive; O. Claytoniana (syn. O. interrupta), a very beautiful species; O. gracilis, Polystichum munitum, Struthiopteris Pennsylvanica, Lomaria Chilensis (Chilian species).

BRITISH.—Athyrium F.f. corymbiferum, a handsome crested variety; A. F.f. Craigii, A. F.f. Elworthii, A. F.f. glomeratum, A. F.f. Grantæ, A. F.f. Howardæ, A. F.f. multifidum, A. F.f. plumosum, a beautiful variety, with large graceful fronds; A. F.f. Pritchardii, a curious variety, with long narrow cruciate fronds; A. F.f. ramo cristatum, A. F.f. rheticum deflexum, pinnules curiously reflexed; A. F.f. setigerum, a very beautiful variety, the fronds having a bristly appearance; A F.f. thyssanotum, A. F.f. todeoides, Lastrea dilatata (the Broad Buckler Fern), L. d. crispato cristata, a pretty variety, with crisp-looking and crested fronds; L. F.m. Barnesii, L. F.m. Bollandiæ, L. F.m. Cronkleyense, L. F.m. digitato Jonesii, L. F.m. grandiceps, very heavily crested; L. F.m. Ingramii, L. F.m. Iveryana, L. F.m. lineare, L. F.m. abbreviata cristata Barnesii, a very distinct and pretty variety; L. pseudomas cristata, a handsome variety, finely crested; L. p.m. cristata angustata, fronds narrow, crimpy, and crested, a distinct variety; L. p.m. Pinderii, L. p.m. polydactyla, an ornamental crested variety; L. spinulosa (the Spiny Buckler Fern), Osmunda regalis (the Royal Fern), one of the largest British Ferns—in a congenial position the fronds often attain a height of six feet; O. r. cristata, a very handsome crested variety, of large growth and pleasing appearance; Polystichum angulare (the soft Prickly Shield Fern), P. a. cristato gracile, P.a. divisilobum, P. a. multilobum (syn. P. a. venustum), a beautiful variety; P. a. proliferum Crawfordianum, Pteris aquilina (the Brake Fern, or Bracken), grows to a large size when planted in a damp, shaded, and sheltered position; P. a. congesta, a peculiarly congested form; P. a. cristata, a crested variety of distinct appearance.

Specially choice species and varieties.

NORTH AMERICAN.—Lastrea fragrans, a dwarf, compact, pretty species, well named "The Violet-scented Fern;" Polystichum acrostichoides grandiceps, a heavily-crested variety, sturdy and compact in habit; Woodsia glabella.

BRITISH.—Asplenium adiantum nigrum acutum, fronds lighter in texture, larger, and more pointed than the species; A. n. grandiceps, bears a comparatively large crest at the apex of each frond; A. Germanicum (syn. alternifolium, the Alternate-leaved Spleenwort); A. septentrionale (the Forked Spleenwort).

Athyrium F.f. acrocladon, fronds much branched, and densely crested, is of compact habit, and very distinct; A. F.f. apicale, a pretty little compact variety, bearing a roundish crest at the apex of each frond; A. F.f. caudigerum, fronds long, narrow, and peculiarly congested; A. F.f. conglomeratum, a nice compact variety, heavily crested; A. F.f. cristulatum, a pretty, dwarf, crested variety; A. F.f. curtum multifidum, a dwarf variety, narrow fronds, crested, specially neat in appearance; A. F.f. Frizellæ coronare, a most beautiful variety of the Frizellæ section, fronds very narrow, and surmounted by a large round yet light-looking crest; A. F.f. Frizellæ gracile, fronds narrow, slender, graceful, divided into two near the bottom; A. F.f. Frizellæ ramo-cristatum, a very pretty variety, fronds branched and crested; A. F.f. gemmatum, very beautiful, fronds two feet long, rather narrow, each pinna and the frond at the tip bearing crisp crests; A. F.f. Girdlestoneii cristatum, a handsome depauperated crested form, light and graceful; A. F.f. Kalothrix, a lovely variety, the foliage very thin in texture, delicate green in colour, finely cut and possessing quite a Filmy-Fern appearance; A. F.f. plumosum elegans, a most beautiful variety, the fronds, one-and-a-half to two feet in length, very pale green, cut into exceedingly fine segments; A. F.f. plumosum multifidum, exceedingly pretty, the fronds light green, finely divided, plumose, and heavily crested; A. F.f. regale, a variety of very handsome appearance, the fronds erect in habit, feathery, and crested; A. F.f. setigerum capitatum, a dwarf variety, possessing the bristly character of *setigerum*, and bearing a small dense crest at the apex of each frond; A. F.f. setigerum percristatum, a strikingly beautiful variety, cristate throughout the whole frond, the crests at the tips of the pinnæ and the end of the frond all arranged in regular order. A. F.f. Victoriæ, often styled "The Queen of the Lady Ferns," is certainly unique. Its fronds attain a length of three feet; the pinnæ arranged along the midrib are very narrow, crested, and in pairs on each side of the stem. They branch at an angle of 45°, one upwards, the other downwards, so that there is a continual series of crossing pinnæ from bottom to top, forming a delicate lattice-work of green frondage. The apex of each frond is crested, the plant has a symmetrical graceful habit, and is very beautiful.

Among these Lady Ferns there are some of the most beautiful Ferns in cultivation, and they will bear comparison with any of the Exotics. Their beauty is most highly developed when cultivated in a cold greenhouse.

Blechnum spicant concinnum, very narrow crimpy fronds; B. s. cristatum, a pretty crested variety; B. s. lineare, fronds long and very narrow, being regularly contracted and neat in appearance; B. s. Maunderii, a densely ramose, crested variety, grows like a green ball.

B. s. plumosum (syn. B. s. serratum, Airey's No. 1), a beautiful variety, with deeply-serrated and sometimes tripinnate fronds, which attain a length of eighteen inches. B. s. trinervo-coronans, a very pretty crested variety, one of the nicest of the genus.

Cystopteris alpina (the Alpine Bladder Fern, syn. C. regia), a handsome species, fronds finely cut.

Lastrea dilatata spectabile, a dwarf and very pretty variety, the fronds finely and distinctly cut; L. pseudomas cristata fimbriata (syn. L. p. m. plumosissima), a very handsome variety, fimbriated, crested, much lighter in appearance than the old *cristata*, compact in habit, graceful, and makes a very pretty specimen. L. p.m. ramosissima, a distinct variety, much branched and crested; L. montana coronans, a beautiful variety, fronds narrow, crested, and compact in habit; L. m. ramocoronans, similar to the preceding, but the fronds branched and the whole appearance of the plant more pleasing.

Polypodium v. Cambricum Prestonii, a beautiful plumose form of the Welsh Polypody; P. v. grandiceps, a heavily crested and very handsome variety; P. v. multifido-cristatum, fronds much branched and crested; P. v. trichomanoides, fronds dense, cut into numberless fine segments, light green, and very pretty.

Polystichum angulare congestum, dense, overlapping foliage; P. a. divisilobum decorum, produces large, broad, drooping fronds, divided into small pinnules; P. a. d. laxum, a very handsome variety, finely divided and graceful; P. a. d. plumosum, one of the most beautiful Ferns in cultivation, the fronds long, very broad at the base, pinnules densely overlapping, producing a moss-like appearance, finely cut, and elegant in the extreme; P. a. foliosa crispum, fronds dense, foliose, and crisp in appearance; P. a. folioso multifidum, a pretty variety, fronds very leafy, crested; P. a. gracile, a very pretty graceful variety; P. a. grandiceps, erect in habit, narrow fronds, bearing a dense crest, very handsome; P. a. Pateyii, a plumose form of considerable beauty; P. a. plumosum, a large and exceedingly handsome plumose variety, makes a grand specimen; P. a. plumoso divisilobum gracile, very beautiful, finely cut, and graceful.

Ferns and Fern Culture. 121

Scolopendrium vulgare crispum fimbriatum, a very beautiful variety, with large, deeply-frilled fronds, fimbriated and dense—one of the most lovely of this family; S. v. crispum robustum, a large and exceedingly handsome form of this pretty variety; S. v. crispum Willsii, a specially pretty broad-fronded variety; S. v. ramo-cristatum majus (Jones), a densely-branched and crested variety, of fine appearance; S. v. ramo-marginatum, a very pretty crested variety, distinct and attractive.

SCOLOPENDRIUM VULGARE RAMO-CRISTATUM MAJUS (JONES).

Of Hardy Ferns, the following are *Evergreen* when protected from the frost: Adiantum capillus veneris and its varieties, Aspidium (in part), Asplenium (in part), Blechnum, Ceterach, Hymenophyllum, Lastrea (in part)), Polypodium (nearly all), Polystichum, Scolopendrium. *Deciduous*: Adiantum pedatum, Allosorus, Aspidium (in part), Asplenium (in part), Athyrium, Botrychium, Cystopteris, Dennstædtia, Onoclea, Ophioglossum, Osmunda, Phegopteris, Polypodium (in part), Pteris, Struthiopteris, Woodsia, Woodwardia.

The species and varieties enumerated in the preceding sections are suitable for borders, beds, or rock ferneries, but the varieties should be selected according to the space at disposal for their development.

SCOLOPENDRIUM VULGARE RAMO-MARGINATUM.

Section 11.

INSECT PESTS.

FERNS are liable to attack from various insect pests. The following are the most common: Scale, Thri s, Green-fly, Black-fly, White-fly, Mealy-bug, Cockroaches, Crickets, Woodlice, Slugs, Snails, and Caterpillars.

Whenever any of these make their appearance means should at once be taken to destroy them. If neglected they quickly multiply, and become much more difficult to eradicate.

Scale, Thrips, Green-fly, Black-fly, White-fly, and Mealy-bug injure the plants by piercing the fronds and sucking out the sap which should support the plant. Cockroaches, Crickets, Woodlice, Slugs, and Snails eat off the young fronds just as they are rising; Slugs are not content with this, but mutilate older fronds; Caterpillars feed upon the developed fronds, sometimes making terrible havoc.

Several kinds of Scale infest Ferns, the commonest being the brown and the white. They attach themselves to the fronds, and have the appearance of small protuberances, brown and hard, or white. When the young emerge from their coverings they are white; they creep along the fronds in large numbers, eventually attaching themselves to a spot where they remain stationary, and proceed to reproduce themselves, meanwhile feeding upon the plant.

Whenever a plant is infested by these it should be carefully cleared of them. They should be rubbed off with the fingers, a pointed stick, or small piece of sponge fastened on the end of a stick. As the foliage is easily injured, the operation must be performed with care. After all that can be seen are removed, the plant should be sponged with warm water, in which a little soft soap has been dissolved. When the plant has plenty of foliage, fronds with a large number of scale on them may be cut off instead of being cleaned, but this must be done judiciously, or unnecessary injury will be done to the plant.

Thrips are exceedingly small insects, white when young, gradually becoming black as they arrive at maturity They are about $\frac{1}{32}$in. in length, with thin bodies, but notwithstanding their smallness they are very destructive. They usually harbour on the under surface of the fronds, but not always. They pierce the cuticle of the frond, and cause great disfigurement to the plant, as well as injury. They attack Hardy Ferns when growing in a house with artificial heat, and plants that are weak and sickly from any cause come in for their special attention.

The most effectual and the easiest mode of destroying these pests is by fumigation several times on alternate nights. This, if strong enough, will destroy most of them for a time, but unfortunately there are many Ferns, particularly Adiantums, which cannot do with fumigation with tobacco paper; therefore, any time this is resorted to, the greatest care will be necessary. One of the safest modes of fumigation is undoubtedly by "Lethorion cones," which are both safe and effectual.

A good plan is to sponge the plants infested, using warm water with a little soft soap dissolved in it, and half as much water added in which quassia chips have been boiled. If the plants are in pots they should be carried out of the fernery while being cleaned, otherwise the thrips will jump off the plant and soon get on others. To eradicate these troublesome creatures considerable patience and perseverance are necessary.

Green-fly harbours on young fronds often, and may be removed by the fingers or a small brush. If very numerous in a house, two or three gentle fumigations will usually destroy them. Another plan is to put a little soft soap in warm water, and beat it into a lather. This may then be put on the Ferns where the fly is located, and it will kill them. This should not be done to Adiantums, but most other kinds liable to these insects may be so treated without injury.

White-fly is rather more troublesome to deal with, as the moment the plant is touched many fly off. Any plant infested should be carefully carried outside and shaken. All that do not fly off may be easily killed, as in the cold air they appear to become stupefied. After all the flies are killed, if the plant be examined there will be seen numbers of tiny white eggs fastened to the fronds. These if not removed will soon hatch and another generation will have to be dealt with. The plant should be sponged as recommended in the case of Thrips, and examined again in two or three days for any that have escaped. When plants infested are planted out and cannot be removed, then either the soft soap lather must be applied or fumigation be resorted to.

Mealy-bug is a peculiar-looking insect, covered with a cotton-wool like substance, very difficult to eradicate when once it gets a firm footing, but fortunately not nearly so common in ferneries as the other pests mentioned. Plants much affected are difficult to clear of it, as again and again it makes its appearance. It is often the wisest course to throw all such into the furnace, fronds and roots as well. Nothing but persistent sponging, picking, and cleaning will be effectual for its destruction. Ferns will not bear the syringing and dipping that hard-wooded stove plants will, hence gentler methods as suggested must be employed.

Cockroaches and Crickets commence their depredations when night comes on, and do most mischief when there is no one there to see them. Traps should be set for these—Birkenhead's Cockroach and Cricket Trap being one of the best. Poison may be laid for them also, and there need be no difficulty in getting rid of them, or at least reducing their numbers, so that those left will be of little consequence. They must not, however, be left undisturbed, even when there are but a few, for, like insects generally, they rapidly multiply, and soon do irreparable mischief.

Woodlice are night raiders, hiding in chinks, holes, under pots, and in other places during the day. Traps should be laid for these. Pieces of turnip, apple, or potato hollowed out, and placed so that they can get in, will often entice them, and they may be caught the next day upon examination of the traps.

Small pots with a little potato in, and filled loosely with moss or hay, placed on their sides near where the insects harbour, will prove very effective traps. They should be examined every morning.

A few toads, notwithstanding the aversion many people have for them, kept in a fernery will destroy a large number of these injurious insects.

Slugs and Snails should be sought for by lamplight. They can rarely be found during the day, although their trail is very conspicuous. About an hour after dark they come out of their hiding places, and may then be caught as they are about to commence further mischief. Sometimes, with the most persistent search, they evade detection. It is then advisable to put down little heaps of bran, saturated with vinegar, and examine them late at night; or lay a few lettuce leaves about, under which they will often creep, and where they may be found the next morning. Hollowed turnips, carrots, and apples serve well as traps. Maidenhair Ferns are terribly pestered by little snails, some with spiral and others with circular shells. These may sometimes be found during the day by looking among the fronds and the crowns of the plants, but being small and dark-coloured they may be easily overlooked. Tiny slugs, after eating the centres out of the young fronds, just as they rise from the crown, often creep into the crowns to hide, and may be found by diligent search. Incessant warfare must be waged against these pests, large and small, or many Ferns will be prevented growing as they otherwise would do.

Caterpillars are very troublesome in the outdoor fernery, and sometimes in cold houses. These must be sought for by daylight and picked off by hand, there being no other way of dealing with them. Another pest which, during the last few years, has made itself very obnoxious to cultivators of plants, is a weevil, dark-coloured and very hard, with roundish body, head prolonged, antennæ bent, and slow in its movements. These creatures are very destructive to hardy Ferns particularly Scolopendriums. They hide during the day, and at night they feed upon the fronds, eating holes in them and pieces out. The greatest mischief, however, is done by the larvæ—white, legless grubs, which work their way among the roots, eating every one they come to. Plants are seen to be drooping, and on examination it is found they are quite loose, the roots underneath being almost completely sheared off. This is only discovered when the mischief is done, and so far there does not appear to be any way of destroying these pests apart from catching them. To accomplish this, the matured insect must be sought for by candlelight; but this must be done very quietly and expeditiously, as the moment the weevils see the light they drop to the ground, remain perfectly motionless, and it is almost impossible to find them. When a plant has been eaten during some night, the culprit may occasionally be found the next day carefully hidden away in the crown, or in a hole near, so that it is always well to be on the look-out. When plants are being repotted there should be a sharp lookout kept for the larvæ; they are easily seen, being white. The eggs, also, may be found in clusters in the soil, and, of course, should be treated in the same manner the more developed larvæ are when they are caught.

Although the insects which are troublesome to the cultivator of Ferns are so numerous, they may be kept down very easily by taking them in hand as soon as they make their appearance. It is when they are allowed to increase, without efforts to restrict them being put forth, that they become so difficult to deal with.

CONCLUSION.

S this treatise deals solely with Ferns, these only have received notice. The best results are attained when Ferns are cultivated in structures specially adapted to their requirements, but many cultivators are unable to provide such, and their Ferns have to grow along with other plants. When this is the case, the Ferns should be placed where they will be least exposed to the sun, and yet receive as much light as is possible. Other plants able to bear strong light may occupy the more exposed positions.

In vineries many Ferns will grow well. During the summer the vines provide shade for the plants below, and during winter, these having lost their foliage, the Ferns receive the unrestricted light, with all of which they can do at that season of the year.

If it be desired to intermix some other plants with Ferns when these are growing in a house devoted mainly to them, ornamental-leaved begonias, palms, and other foliage plants will be found to associate harmoniously with them. For covering rockwork the pretty, ivy-like, clinging Ficus repens, the smaller and neater-looking Ficus minima, and small-leaved green and variegated Ivies are admirably suited. As trailing plants to hang over ledges of rocks and clothe the surface of the soil, Sibthorpia Europea, its beautiful though somewhat delicate-looking variegated variety, Tradescantias, Isolepis gracilis, and similar plants, are not to be surpassed.

Flowering plants, usually, are not desirable, and such as produce gaudy, showy flowers are objectionable.

Masses of colour, brilliant and dazzling as they sometimes are, may be quite in place elsewhere, but not in the fernery. There the delightful refreshing greenery should afford rest to the eye, and allow the sight to wander from plant to plant, taking in all their unassuming and unobtrusive beauty without the weariness frequently produced by the glaring colours exhibited in the flowers of some other plants.

JOHN HEYWOOD, Excelsior Printing & Bookbinding Works, Hulme Hall Road, Manchester.

A VALUABLE PUBLICATION.

The largest, most beautiful, useful, interesting and profusely

Illustrated Catalogue

OF

FERNS & SELAGINELLAS

EVER PUBLISHED (No. 22.)

It contains **150** fine Illustrations (many of them full page), which give an admirable idea of the habit and appearance of the various species represented.

It also gives many synonyms of the Ferns, the countries of which they are natives; the average height to which they grow; many descriptions, together with a large amount of interesting matter of various kinds, constituting it a highly valuable book for every Fern lover.

Price **TWO SHILLINGS**, Post Free.

W. & J. BIRKENHEAD,

Fern Nurseries,

SALE, MANCHESTER.

Collections of FERNS & SELAGINELLAS

(W. & J. B.'s SELECTION),

For STOVE, WARM, COOL or COLD GREENHOUSE.

12 different kinds		4/-	larger	6/-	9/-	12/-
25 do. do.		10/6	,,	15/-	21/-	25/-
50 do. do.		25/-	,,	35/-	50/-	63/-
100 in 50 different kinds...		50/-	,,	63/-	75/-	84/-
100 in 100 do. do.		70/-	,,	84/-	105/-	126/-
12 Hardy Exotic, different kinds				6/-	9/-	12/-
25 do. do. do. do.				21/-	30/-	35/-
12 Hardy Exotic and British		3/-		4/-	6/-	9/-
25 do. do.		10/6		15/-	21/-	25/-
50 do. do.		30/-		50/-	63/-	75/-
100 do. in 50 kinds		50/-		63/-	75/-	84/-
100 do. in 100 do.		84/-		105/-	126/-	150/-
6 different kinds for Dwelling House		3/-		4/6	6/-	9/-
6 do. do. for Fern Stands or Cases ...		2/-		3/-	6/-	9/-
12 do. do. do. do. ...		6/-		9/-	12/-	18/-
25 do. do. do. do. ...		15/-		21/-	25/-	35/-
12 do. do. for Window Cases		4/-		6/-	9/-	12/-
12 do. do. for Window Boxes		3/-		4/-	6/-	9/-
6 do. do. for Baskets...		3/-		6/-	9/-	12/-
12 do. do. do.		12/-		18/-	24/-	30/-
Ferns on Cork for Suspending ... ...each		1/6		2/6	3/6	5/-

HARDY BRITISH FERNS FOR ROCKERIES, &c.

Strong, well-rooted Plants, in 8 of the larger, and, if desired, in 6 or 8 of the smaller growing species ... ... **20/- per hundred.**

Disappointment is often experienced when recently collected, low-priced Plants are bought. Sometimes they are very small, at other times almost destitute of roots, and rarely do any good. It is much better to pay a little more for such Plants as are offered above, which always give satisfaction.

W. & J. BIRKENHEAD,
FERN NURSERIES, SALE, Manchester.

REQUISITES FOR FERN CULTURE.

COMPOST, consisting of loam, leaf-mould and sand, in their proper proportions ready for use. One Bushel Sack, 2/6; Two Bushel Sack, 4/6.

COMPOST, consisting of loam, leaf-mould, sand and peat. One Bushel Sack, 2/6; Two Bushel Sack, 4/6.

COMPOST, consisting of loam, leaf-mould, silver sand, peat and Charcoal, for the choicest varieties. One Bushel Sack, 3/-; Two Bushel Sack, 5/6.

LOAM, of excellent quality. One Bushel Sack, 2/-; Two Bushel Sack, 3/6.

LEAF MOULD of finest quality. One Bushel Sack, 3/-; Two Bushel Sack, 5/6.

PEAT, best quality. One Bushel Sack, 3/6; Two Bushel Sack, 6/6.

SILVER SAND (coarse, the best for Ferns). One Bushel Sack, 4/-.

CHARCOAL, in large pieces or fine. One Bushel Sack, 2/6; Two Bushel Sack, 4/6.

GREEN WOOD MOSS. One Bushel Sack, 3/-; Two Bushel Sack, 5/6.

SPHAGNUM MOSS. One Bushel Sack, 4/-; Two Bushel Sack, 7/6.

SANDSTONE, broken small. One Bushel Sack, 2/6.

N.B.—For every Sack returned in good condition, carriage paid, 6d. each will be allowed.

VIRGIN CORK, 20/- per cwt., 11/- per ½-cwt, 6/- per ¼-cwt.

W. & J. BIRKENHEAD,
Fern Nurseries, SALE, Manchester.

THE BEST PLACE TO PROCURE FERNS.

LETHORION (VAPOUR CONE).

PATENT.

They are now universally admitted to be thoroughly uniform in strength and safe for any plant or flower, even if four times the quantity are used. Scale and mealy-bug may be completely eradicated by using the Cones double strength.

PRICES:

For frames of 50 to 100 cubic feet,
No. 1, reduced to........ 6d. each
500 feet, No. 2 ....1s. 0d. ,,
1,000 feet, No. 3 ....1s. 6d. ,,
4,000 feet, No. 4 ....5s. 0d. ,,

The house should be well secured.

CORRY & CO., LIMITED,
13, 15 and 16, FINSBURY STREET, LONDON, E.C.

Sold by Messrs. W. & J. BIRKENHEAD, Fern Nursery SALE,
and all Seedsmen and Florists.

("THE 'TIMES' OF HORTICULTURE.")

3d.] A WEEKLY ILLUSTRATED JOURNAL. [3d.
Established 1841.
EVERY FRIDAY. THE OLDEST HORTICULTURAL NEWSPAPER.

THE "GARDENERS' CHRONICLE" has been for *over fifty years* the leading journal of its class. It has achieved this position because, while specially devoting itself to supplying the daily requirements of gardeners of all classes, much of the information furnished is of such general and *permanent value*, that the "Gardeners' Chronicle" is looked up to as the *standard authority* on the subjects on which it treats.

CIRCULATION.—Its relations with amateur and professional gardeners and with the Horticultural Trade of all countries, are of a specially extensive character, and its circulation is constantly increasing.

CONTRIBUTORS.—Its contributors comprise the leading British gardeners and many of the most eminent men of science at home and abroad.

ILLUSTRATIONS.—The "Gardeners' Chronicle" has obtained an International reputation for the accuracy, permanent utility and artistic effect of its illustrations of plants. These illustrations, together with the original articles and monographs, render the "Gardeners' Chronicle" an indispensable work of reference in all garden reading rooms and botanical libraries.

SUPPLEMENTS.—Double-page engravings, lithographs, and other illustrations of large size, are frequently given as Supplements, without extra charge.

ALL SUBSCRIPTIONS PAYABLE IN ADVANCE.

The United Kingdom:—12 months, 15s.; 6 months, 7s. 6d.; 3 months, 3s. 9d. Post free.

All Foreign subscriptions, including Postage, 17s. 6d. for 12 months

Post Office Orders to be made payable at the Post Office, 42, DRURY LANE, London, to A. G. MARTIN.

Cheques should be crossed "DRUMMOND." Telegraphic Address—GARDCHRON, LONDON.

Office:—41, WELLINGTON STREET, STRAND, LONDON, W.C.

⁎⁎⁎ May be ordered of all Booksellers and Newsagents, and at the Railway Bookstalls.

A WONDERFUL BEETLE TRAP.

2,000 COCKROACHES
CAUGHT IN ONE NIGHT IN ONE OF
BIRKENHEAD'S BEETLE TRAPS.

ARE YOU TROUBLED BY
Cockroaches, Black Beetles, Crickets?

IF SO, YOU SHOULD OBTAIN ONE OR MORE OF
BIRKENHEAD'S
COCKROACH, CRICKET & BEETLE TRAPS.
Always ready for use, without further expense, after the first small outlay.
1/6 each; per Parcel Post, 2/-.

Ask your Ironmonger or Seedsman for them, or write to
W. & J. BIRKENHEAD,
Inventors and Manufacturers, **FERN NURSERY, SALE, MANCHESTER.**

THE ADVANTAGE. BIRKENHEAD'S TRAPS have OVER ALL OTHERS is, that they may be placed in a corner of the room, cupboard, or other place, and, fitting close to the wall, are more effectual than other Traps of different shape. There is no TIN TO RUST, WIRE TO BEND, or anything else to get out of order.

The following are selected from a large number of similar unsolicited Testimonials.
A gentleman had five Traps from us, and writing afterwards, says: "The Traps were *very* successful; **one Trap** caught last night no less than **2,000**."
Writing again several days after, he sent a further remittance, saying: "As all the Traps I am now getting are to give away (as I think I am giving a really useful article) will you send one to each of the four following addresses."
A gentleman sending a second order writes: "In **one night** I caught **1,570** Beetles in **one Trap** in the stoke-hole of my greenhouse, and **1,074** in another in the kitchen. I have caught great numbers since, but have not taken the trouble to count them."

SPECIAL NOTICE.

IF YOU WANT
REALLY GOOD BULBS AND SEEDS
AT MODERATE PRICES, APPLY TO

Mr. Robert Sydenham,
Of the Firm of Sydenham Brothers, Wholesale Jewellers
TENBY STREET, BIRMINGHAM,
THE LARGEST AMATEUR IMPORTER IN THE KINGDOM.

HIS
UNIQUE BULB LIST
WITH PAMPHLET, NOW REVISED AND ENLARGED,
"HOW I CAME TO GROW BULBS,"
The Most Reliable Guide to the Best Varieties,
and How to Grow them.

SENT POST FREE ON APPLICATION.
Mr. SYDENHAM'S Hyacinths were represented, and gained best Prizes at London, Birmingham, Preston, Shrewsbury, &c., &c., in 1891 and 1892.

ALL SHOULD HAVE HIS
UNIQUE SEED LIST
Which is acknowledged to be the Best, Cheapest, Most Reliable, and Unique List ever published; it contains only the
BEST VEGETABLES AND FLOWERS,
WORTH GROWING,
Being the selections of the largest Seed Growers, the largest Market Gardeners, and the most Celebrated Professional Gardeners and Amateurs in the Kingdom; it contains most useful cultural instructions for Amateurs. Published in December.

POST FREE ON APPLICATION.

HIS ORIGINAL GUARANTEE,
SUCH AS NEVER OFFERED BY THE TRADE.

ALL BULBS which fail under fair and proper treatment WILL BE REPLACED THE FOLLOWING SEASON AT HALF PRICE. ALL SEEDS from which a fair proportion fail to germinate under fair and proper treatment WILL BE REPLACED FREE. Notice of failure should be given at once.

WILLESDEN MANUFACTURES.

Awarded Seven Gold and Eight Silver Medals.

WILLESDEN ROT-PROOF SCRIM.

For SHADING Greenhouses, Ferneries, protection of Tender Plants, and various Horticultural, Manufacturing, and other purposes.

		WHITE.		GREEN.	
F T O	open	1s. 1d. per yard run.		1s. 0d. per yard run.	
A L F	close	1s. 7d.	,,	1s. 6d.	,,
F T	,,	1s. 7d.	,,	1s. 6d.	,,
A L F B	,,	1s. 7½d.	,,	1s. 6½d.	,,

55 inches wide (approx.)

Repeat order from His Grace the Duke of Marlborough:
" I herewith enclose you order for 300 yards Willesden Scrim Shading *the same as before—* On account of His Grace the Duke of Marlborough, Blenheim Gardens, Woodstock.— April 24th, 1891."
" I am most satisfied with my previous purchase of this article."—GEO. FELLOWS, Esq., Nottingham.
" Your Scrim gives great satisfaction."—R. P. BARBER, Esq., Hounslow.
"I have some of the Scrim in use, and it has answered admirably and wears well."— Rev. THOS. CARROLL, Netley, Hants.
" Very durable, and quite worth the additional expense over the ordinary material."— C. H. GOODMAN, Esq., Wandsworth.
"The Scrim is as good as new now."—F. D. CAMPBELL, Esq., Eastbourne.
" Your Rot-proof Scrim is very durable "—Sir LUSHINGTON PHILLIPS, Kingsbridge.
" I take this opportunity of saying how much pleased I am with the Scrim for shading Orchid Houses. I had my blinds up all the Winter, so as to use them on cold nights, and have found them most useful, and they wear well."—JOHN DUKE, Esq., M.D., Lewisham.
" I have used your Scrim for Greenhouse Blinds, and it is as good now as the first day it was put up (four years ago). I have recommended it to many friends."— S. H. C. KINGSFORD, Esq., Patent Office.
WILLESDEN ROT-PROOF CANVAS, for all purposes and all climates.
WILLESDEN ROOFING (4-ply). 9d. per yard run, 19 in. wide. Lord Egerton of Tatton has found that Cattle under Sheds Roofed with Willesden Roofing do better than under Slate Roofs, which he attributes to the fact that it is cooler in Summer and warmer in Winter.—See the *Globe*, Monday, December 8, 1884.
WILLESDEN PAPER (2-ply and 1-ply), for underlinings, damp walls, etc.

WILLESDEN PAPER AND CANVAS WORKS,

Willesden Junction, N.W.,

London Depôt:—51, BOW LANE, E.C.

Liverpool Depôt:—43, SOUTH JOHN STREET.

WILLIAM COOPER'S HORTICULTURAL APPLIANCES.

AMATEUR GREENHOUSE.

Made in sections, so that any gardener or handy man can erect with facility in a few hours. Simply screwed together. 7ft. by 5ft., 56/-; 9ft. by 6ft., £4; 12ft. by 8ft., £6; 15ft. by 10ft., £8 10s.; 20ft. by 10ft., £12; 25ft. by 10ft., £17.

ANY SIZE MADE.

Cucumber Frames.

THE ONLY PERFECT PROPAGATOR
For Raising Plants from Seeds, Slips, or Cuttings.

One-light Frames, 4ft. by 3ft., 18s.; ditto, 6ft. by 4ft., £1 10s. Two-light Frames, 6ft. by 4ft., £1 12s.; ditto, 8ft. by 6ft., £2 14s. Three-light Frames, 12ft. by 6ft., £3 15s.

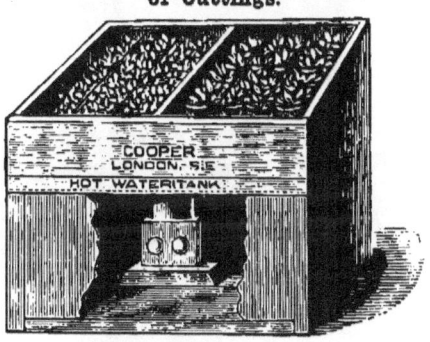

COMPLETE FROM 25/-

HORTICULTURAL
GLASS—GLASS—GLASS.

10,000 Boxes to select from.

	15oz., 100ft.	21oz., 100ft.	15oz., 200ft.	21oz., 200ft.
4th.	8s. 9d.	12s. 0d.	17s. 0d.	24s. 0d.
3rd.	10s. 0d.	13s. 6d.	19s. 0d.	26s. 6d.

All sizes in stock. Glass cut to any size required: 15oz., 1½d. per ft.; 21oz., 2½d. per ft. Large sizes for cutting up: 15oz., per case 300ft., 26s.; 21oz., per case 200ft., 26s. All glass is cut and packed in own warehouses; quality of glass and careful packing guaranteed. Special quotations given for large quantities. Have cash estimate from me before ordering elsewhere.
PUTTY prepared especially for greenhouse work, 7s. cwt.

GARDEN LIGHTS.

4ft. by 3ft., 6/6.
6ft. by 4ft., 9/-.

PAINTED, AND GLAZED WITH 21oz.

WILLIAM COOPER,
Horticultural Provider,

SEND FOR LIST.   747 to 755, OLD KENT ROAD, LONDON, S.E.

William Cooper's Heating Apparatus.

COOPER'S IMPROVED
AMATEUR HYGIENIC HEATER.

For Burning Paraffin Oil or Gas without Smoke or Smell.

These Heaters are constructed as a means of heating by Hot Air without the use of Hot Water or Fires. Its peculiar construction economises the Heat generated, so that there is no waste of Heat or Fuel. There being perfect combustion in this Stove, and nothing whatever injurious to Plants, but actually everything conducive to their health, it should be observed that Plants may be had in full bloom throughout the severest Winter. This cannot be obtained in Stoves of other systems.

Carefully packed and put on rail at the following prices:—

							£	s.	d.		£	s.	d.
No. 0 will heat House 7ft. by 5		consumes ⅜ Pt. Oil in 10 hrs.		1	0	0	extra for gas	2	0	
No. 1	,,	9ft. by 6	,,	1	,,		1	10	0	,,	2	0
No. 2	,,	12ft. by 8	,,	1¼	,,		2	5	0	,,	3	0
No. 3	,,	15ft. by 10	,,	2	,,		3	5	0	,,	5	0
No. 4	,,	20ft. by 10	,,	3	,,		3	10	0	,,	12	0
No. 5	,,	25ft. by 10	,,	4	,,		4	0	0	,,		

THE "INVINCIBLE" HOT WATER APPARATUS.
(TENANT'S FIXTURE.)

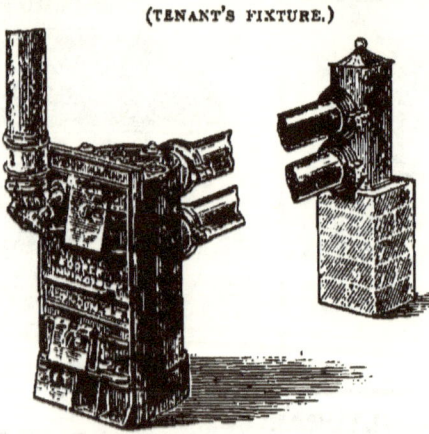

PORTABLE AND COMPLETE.

FITTED WITH IRON CHIMNEYS.

This is the simplest, cheapest, and most powerful Hot Water Apparatus made.
Cost of complete Apparatus for Greenhouses with 4in. pipes, flow and return along one side cut and fitted; so that if the internal measurement of the Greenhouse is given, the Apparatus will be delivered completely ready for fixing, an advantage which will be appreciated by all.

Securely packed and forwarded carriage paid to any station in the United Kingdom at the following respective prices:—

10ft. by 7ft.	12ft. by 8ft.	15ft. by 10ft.	20ft. by 10ft.	25ft. by 10ft.	50ft. by 10ft.
£5 0 0	£5 10 0	£6 10 0	£7 12 0	£8 5 0	£12 15 0

The following are extra: Set of Stoking Tools, 5s.; Cap to Stove Pipe, if required, 1s. 6d.

N.B.—PRICES OF ABOVE ARE NOW REDUCED 20 PER CENT.

For other Apparatus see List, post free.

WILLIAM COOPER,
747 to 755, OLD KENT ROAD, LONDON, S.E.

WILLIAM COOPER'S MANURES.

Manures—Various.

Orchid Peat, 6/- per sack, 5 for 25/-, 10 for 45/.
Best Brown Fibrous Peat, 2/6 per sack, 6 for 13/-, 10 for 20/-
Good General Peat, 2/- per sack, 6 for 10/-, 10 for 15/-
Rhododendron Peat, 2/- per sack, 6 for 10/-, 10 for 15/-
Rich Brown Loose Peat, 2/- per sack, 6 for 10/-, 10 for 15/-
Cocoanut Fibre Refuse, 9d. per sack, 10 for 7/-, 15 for 10/-, 20 for 13/-, 30 for 20/-
Best Peruvian Guano, 16/- per cwt.
Nitrate of Soda, 14/- per cwt.
Sulphate of Ammonia, 17/- per cwt.
Nitrate of Potash, 18/- per cwt.
Kainit, 6/- per cwt.
Superphosphate, 6/6 per cwt.
Charcoal nuts or fine, 4/6 per sack, 6 for 24/-, 10 for 36/-

Silver Sand, 1/4 per cwt., all sacks free.
Loam, Surrey, splendid quality, 2/6 per sack, 5 for 11/-, 10 for 20/-
General Potting Compost, 2/6 per sack, 6 for 13/-, 10 for 20/-
Prepared Compost for Potting Ferns, 2/6 per sack, 6 for 13/-, 10 for 20/-
Prepared Compost for Potting Bulbs, 2/6 per sack, 6 for 13/-, 10 for 20/-
Leaf Soil, well decayed, 2/6 per sack, 6 for 13/-, 10 for 20/-
Pure Dry Blood, 15/- per cwt.
Dissolved Bone Compound, 9/- per cwt.
Bone Flour, 9/6 per cwt.
Bone Meal, 9/6 per cwt.
Half-inch Bones, 8/6 per cwt.
Superphosphate of Lime, 7/- per cwt

COOPER'S WONDERFUL NEW MUSHROOM SPAWN.

Very best quality, producing abundant Crops of Superior Fleshy Mushrooms.

1 bushel— 16 bricks	....	4/-
7 ,, 112 ,,	....	25/-
14 ,, 244 ,,	....	45/-
28 ,, 488 ,,	....	80/-

For full Directions for Growing, see List.

WILLIAM COOPER'S FUMIGATING INSECTICIDE

CERTAIN DEATH TO INSECT PESTS.

Two or three of these suspended by a wire under a greenhouse stage, and lighted at each end, will quickly settle the accounts of the green fly and thrips, and that with comparatively little trouble. Success guaranteed. 6d. each; 6 for 2s. 6d., 4s. 6d. per doz., 6 doz. 20s., 35s. per gross.

WILLIAM COOPER'S "GENERAL" FERTILIZER.

Tins, 4d.; 7lb. Bags, 1s.; 14lb. Bags, 2s.

This high-class Manure is strongly recommended for all kinds of Flowers, Fruit Trees, and Vegetables; and will be found invaluable both for improving and increasing the produce. Suitable for all Crops.

WILLIAM COOPER'S WORM DESTROYER.

Invaluable for destroying Worms on Tennis Courts, Cricket Grounds, Bowling Greens and Lawns, or removing them from the roots of Plants in Pots. Prices: In bottles, 1s. 6d. and 3s.; per gallon, 7s.; quantities over 5 gallons, 5s. per gallon.

WILLIAM COOPER'S SUNSHADE.

SUPERSEDES ALL OTHER PREPARATIONS OF THE KIND.

The cheapest, most efficient, and convenient preparation for Shading Greenhouses, Conservatories, Glass Roofs, and Windows of all descriptions. Prices in Tins, 1lb., 6d.; 2lb., 1s.; 7lb., 3s. 6d.

WILLIAM COOPER'S WEED DESTROYER.

MY OWN MANUFACTURE.

For permanently destroying Vegetation on Walks, Carriage Drives, &c. Prices: In cane and casks: 1 gal., 2/-; 5 gals, 1/6 per gal.; 10 gals., 1/4 per gal.; 20 gals., 1/3 per gal.; 40 gals., 1/- per gal.

WILLIAM COOPER'S INSECTICIDE.

Is the most Effective, the Safest, and the Cheapest Insect Destroyer. One gallon of this Insecticide will make 200 gallons of efficient wash. Price in bottles: ½ pint, 6d.; 1 pint, 1/-; 1 quart, 1/6; ½ gallon, 3/-; 1 gallon, 5/- special price for large quantities.

For other Manures, &c., See List, Post Free.

W. COOPER, HORTICULTURAL PROVIDER,
747 to 755, OLD KENT ROAD, LONDON, S.E.

GREENHOUSE MATERIALS.
W. COOPER,
HORTICULTURAL PROVIDER,
747 to 755, Old Kent Road, LONDON, E.C.

THOROUGHLY WELL-SEASONED YELLOW DEAL SASHBAR.

1¼in. by 1in.	£0	3	9	Per 100ft. Run.
2in. ,, 1in.	0	4	6	,,
2½in. ,, 1in.	0	6	6	,,
3in. ,, 1½in.	0	8	6	,,

Pit Light Stile and Top Rail.

2½in. ,, 1½in.	£0	9	6	,,
2in. ,, 2in.	0	10	6	,,
3in. ,, 2in.	0	12	6	,,

Prepared Quartering.

4¼in. ,, 3in.	£1	5	0	,,
3in. ,, 3in.	0	15	0	,,
3in. ,, 2in.	0	12	0	,,
3in. ,, 1½in.	0	10	0	,,
3in. ,, 1in.	0	7	0	,,

Prepared Sills, 7in. by 2¼in., 3½d. per foot Run.
Ridges, Grooved, 7in. by 1¼in., 2½d. per foot Run.
Half Glass Doors, 5ft 6in. by 2ft. 6in., 8s. 6d. each.
Do.   do.   6ft. by 2ft. 6in., 9s. 6d. each.
Top or Side Ventilators, 2ft. 6in. by 2ft., 2s. 6d. each.
¾in. Beads, 1s. 9d. per 100ft. Run.
⅝in. Matchboards, Tongued, Grooved, and
    Beaded ... ... 6s. 6d. ⎫
¾in. Ditto   do.   do. ... ...   12s.   ⎬ Per 100ft. super
1in. Ditto   do.   do. ... ...   15s.   ⎪
1in. Yellow Floorboards ... ...10s. 6d. ⎭

Special Quotations given for Large Quantities, and all other materials required for Building Greenhouses, &c., &c.

SANKEY'S
"SPECIAL CHRYSANTHEMUM POTS"

SANKEY'S
"SPECIAL TOMATO POTS"

SANKEY'S
"SPECIAL VINE POTS"

"ORCHID POTS"

PANS,
&c.

LARGEST MANUFACTURERS IN THE WORLD.

Carriage and Breakage free on £10 orders; half carriage on £5 orders.

AGENTS IN NEARLY ALL PARTS OF THE UNITED KINGDOM.

Where no Agents Sankey's quote for
☞ **SMALL QUANTITIES DELIVERED FREE.** ☜
SAMPLES AND PRICES FREE.

The Great ROSE, DAHLIA and VINE GROWERS.

KEYNES, WILLIAMS & CO.,
THE NURSERIES,
SALISBURY.

CATALOGUES GRATIS.

TWENTY-FIVE AWARDS OF MERIT.
Used in the Royal Gardens.

ESPECIALLY ADAPTED FOR THE CULTIVATION OF
FLOWERS, FRUITS & VEGETABLES.

FOR FERNS

THE ONE THING NEEDFUL

FOR FERNS

In Packets, 1lb., 6d.; 2lbs., 1/-; 7lbs., 2/6; *Postage Extra*
Also in Bags, 14lbs., 4/6; 28lbs., 7/6; 56lbs., 12/6; 112lbs., 20/-; *Carriage Paid.*

REGISTERED

Of Nurserymen, Seedsmen, Florists and Chemists,
OR DIRECT FROM
WILLIAM COLCHESTER, IPSWICH.

GARDEN-WORK
(ILLUSTRATED).

WEEKLY—ONE PENNY.

A Paper for the Million, which should be obtained by all who take pleasure in having a good supply of

FLOWERS, FRUITS, AND VEGETABLES.

THE BEST, MOST PRACTICAL AND USEFUL ILLUSTRATED PENNY GARDENING PAPER IN THE WORLD.

[EVERY AMATEUR IN TOWN OR COUNTRY SHOULD OBTAIN A COPY.]

GARDEN-WORK

May be obtained of any Bookseller, Stationer, or at any of the Railway Bookstalls. Annual Subscription, 6s. 6d. A First-class Medium for Advertisers.

WHAT THE PRESS SAYS:—

"'GARDEN-WORK' will worthily fill the appropriate niche. It is an excellent pennyworth, and we do not think that those who invest in this pennyworth of wisdom will run the slightest chance of being 'pound foolish.'"—*Gardeners' Chronicle.*

"Promises to be useful to tens of thousands who care much for plain common-sense gardening, and its price (1d.) should carry it into every household where a garden paper is likely to find a welcome."—*Gardeners' Magazine.*

"Contains a vast amount of pleasant reading and practical information for those who possess even the smallest strip of garden ground."—*Times.*

"A charming paper. Every page is written in simple style, and there is an entire absence of inaccurate scientific jargon that is too common in many journals."—*Morning Post.*

"Really a first-rate piece of journalistic composition. We have no doubt this new venture will have an extensive circulation."—*Literary World.*

"'GARDEN-WORK' is, we think, the best of its class that has appeared, and would be very useful for amateurs, as well as for those more experienced in horticultural matters."—*Weekly Budget.*

EDW. H. MAY, Publisher.   Office: 171, Fleet St., London, E.C.

'KENT, the GARDEN OF ENGLAND.'

600,000 FRUIT TREES TRUE TO NAME.

THE GRANDEST STOCK IN EUROPE.

BOTH MARKET AND GARDEN TREES,
VERY CLEAN AND WELL TRAINED.

WALL, ORCHARD-HOUSE TREES, FIGS, VINES, &c.

The New Descriptive Illustrated List, 6 Stamps.   Reference List Gratis.

NEW STRAWBERRY CATALOGUE IN JULY.

LIBERAL TERMS, FREE CARRIAGE, and CASH DISCOUNTS.

GEORGE BUNYARD & CO.,
THE OLD NURSERIES, MAIDSTONE.

Also 40 ACRES FOREST TREES, ROSES, SHRUBS, and CONIFERS, in Splendid Order for Removal.   List free.

By Royal Letters Patent.

WEEKS'S PATENT
Duplex Compensating Upright Tubular Boiler

For Heating Conservatories, Vineries, Greenhouses, Churches, Chapels, Schools, Billiard Rooms, Warehouses, &c.,

Offers advantages totally unheard of, and unapproached by any of its contemporaries

THE ONLY INDESTRUCTIBLE BOILER.

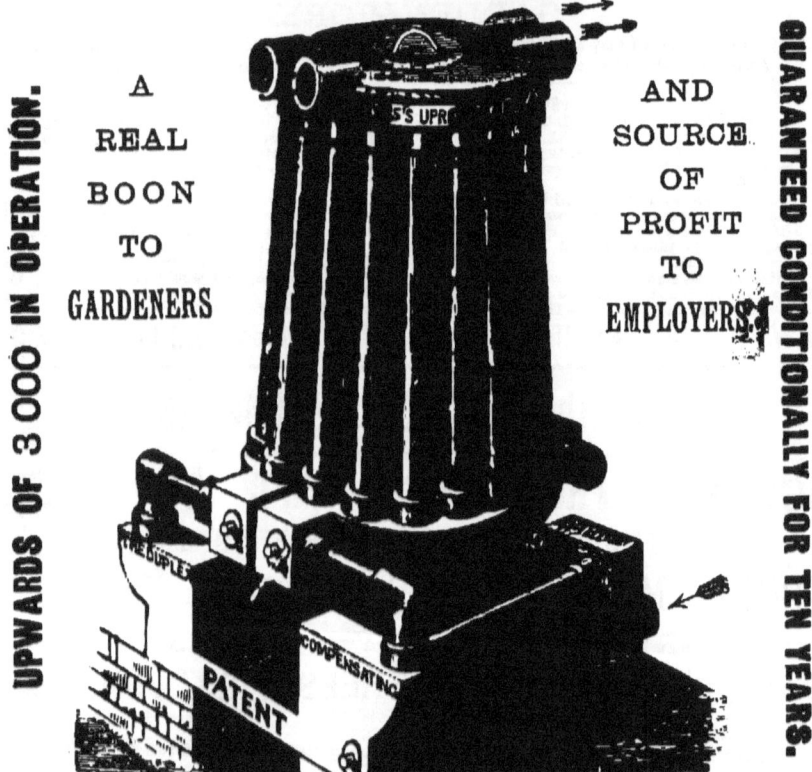

A REAL BOON TO GARDENERS

AND SOURCE OF PROFIT TO EMPLOYERS.

UPWARDS OF 3000 IN OPERATION.

GUARANTEED CONDITIONALLY FOR TEN YEARS.

Conservatories, Orchid Houses, and all garden structures of BEST WORKMANSHIP & MATERIALS ONLY.

For full particulars and Lithographs of Boilers, also 15th ENLARGED EDITION of Illustrated Catalogue and particulars of their new Hydro-Caloric Warming and Ventilating Apparatus, post free, apply to —

J. WEEKS & CO.,
Horticultural Builders and Hot-Water Apparatus Manufacturers,
KING'S ROAD, CHELSEA, S.W.

THE GARDENING WORLD

ESTABLISHED 1884.

The Leading Gardening Paper.

PUBLISHED EVERY THURSDAY FOR SATURDAY,
Price ONE PENNY; Post Free, THREE-HALFPENCE.

A FIRST-CLASS MEDIUM FOR ADVERTISING.

Subscription payable in advance, Three Months, 1s. 8d.;
Six Months, 3s. 3d.; Twelve Months, 6s. 6d.

PUBLISHING OFFICE:—

1, CLEMENT'S INN, STRAND, LONDON, W.C.

THE "STOTT"
HORTICULTURAL SPECIALITIES.

PATENT DISTRIBUTOR, 28/- complete.
PATENT SPRAYER, 4/- and 5/- each.
PATENT INSECTICIDE SYRINGE, with Patent Sprayer, 21/- each.

KILLMRIGHT.
Best, safest Insecticide for garden pests and eradication of mildew.

FEEDMRIGHT.
BEST FERTILIZER FOR ALL PLANT LIFE.
Write for Price Lists. 2 oz. Sample Killmright free on application.

THE "STOTT" DISTRIBUTOR CO. LD.,
Barton House, Manchester.

HARDEMAN'S
GREENHOUSE INSECTICIDE
AND CELEBRATED
WOODLICE EXTERMINATOR.

NON-POISONOUS.   (REGISTERED.)   NON-POISONOUS.

Harmless to Plants,

And specially recommended to growers of Mushrooms, Cucumbers & Ferns.

BELLOWS FOR DISTRIBUTION OF THE POWDER.

Destroys WOODLICE, THRIPS, GREEN FLY, ANTS, BEETLES, CRICKETS.

To Re-fill Bellows remove small Cork at bottom.

Sold in tin dredgers, 6d., 1/-, 2/6, 5/-; and in bulk of 1-lb., 3-lb., 5-lb., and 7-lb. cases. Bellows, 1/- each, filled, free by post for 1/2.

ALSO THE FOLLOWING REQUISITES FOR GREENHOUSE USE:

PLANT SOAP, FLOWER CEMENT,
INDELIBLE INK for Wood Labels, ZINC LABEL INK, &c.

Beetles & Crickets, however numerous, destroyed in a few nights.

HARDEMAN'S CELEBRATED
LONDON BEETLE POWDER
AND UNIVERSAL INSECT DESTROYER.

NON-POISONOUS.   (REGISTERED.)   NON-POISONOUS.

DESTROYS BEETLES, CRICKETS, BUGS, FLEAS, WOODLICE, GREEN FLY, ANTS, MOTHS.

☞ Sold in packets, 3d., 6d., 1s., 2s. 6d., 5s.; and in bulk of 3-lb., 5-lb. and 7-lb. Also in tin dredgers to suit purchasers. Bellows filled 1s. each.

Sold by Chemists, Ironmongers, and Seedsmen in all towns throughout the United Kingdom.

"Greater Fleas have little Fleas upon their legs to bite 'em,
And little Fleas have lesser Fleas, and so *ad infinitum*."

Sole Proprietor: **JOHN HARDEMAN,**
Works: Lloyd St., Moulton St., Strangeways, MANCHESTER.
Retail Depot: 59, Bury New Road, MANCHESTER.

PORTER'S
PATENT INVINCIBLE CROCK
FOR PLANT POTS.

Keeps out worms and all vermin.

Saves time, expense, and annoyance.

Fits any pot.

Lasts for many years.

They are made f brass.

Do not in any way interfere with the ordinary drainage, nor with the outlet of surplus water.

Mr. B. GILBERT, Gardener to the MARQUIS OF EXETER, writes:—"I look upon your brass Crock for keeping out worms as one of those simple and practical inventions we stand so much in need of. I feel sure I am speaking the sentiments of all my brothers in arms when I say we owe you a debt of gratitude."

Mr. E. S. DODWELL, Oxford, writes:—"I think very highly of your Invincible Crock; there can be no doubt about its usefulness. For keeping worms and all other vermin out of plant pots, nothing can be better."

T. BROOKS, Esq., Barkly Hall, Leicester, writes:—"Please send me another 300 Invincible Crocks. They are splendid. Have long been wanted."

They are sent out in two sizes, mixed.

The illustration shows the small size, which suits small and medium sized pots.

The large size suits all larger pots.

30...1/-   100...3/-   1,000...25/-   Post Free.

A. PORTER, STONE HOUSE, MAIDSTONE.
TESTIMONIALS AND PRESS OPINIONS FREE.

www.ingramcontent.com/pod-product-compliance
Lightning Source LLC
Chambersburg PA
CBHW022128160426
43197CB00009B/1193